Management Pearls (Purls) and other tidbits I have Learned Along the Way

George A Humphrey, Ph.D.

Acknowledgments

The author wishes to thank God, who is the head of his life, for allowing me to make it to this milestone.

The author wishes to thank all the members of the Biloxi L269 Course back in 2009. You are the inspiration for this book. Those of you include J Griffiths, Pace, Gina; Bridges, Sterling; Billups, Teresa; Trzaska, Andrea; Reyes, Mark A; McDonnell, Jill, Treadaway, James; Forero, Jaime; Gautier, Caroline B; Phelps, Margaret; Vacroux, Nathalie A; Strouse, Philip A; Brezany, Eugene; Cvitanovich, Yvette; Hurley, Elizabeth T; Chidester, Christopher; Windham, Jason F; Meyer, Joan; Gardner, William; Humphrey, George A; Anderson, Valerie; Hill, Marcia L; Woods, Yolanda M; Allen, Leann M; Langlinais, Kenneth M; Mcgee, Darryl; antronia.johnson@fema.gov; Wilson, Gregory P; Haywood, Robert A; Peter Vaslow; Collins, Lucille

The author wishes to thank all his family and friends, church family, work family and all who have had an impact on his life.

The author wishes to thank his sons, George II and Darion, for their love and support.

The author wishes to thank his siblings, Victor, Robert, Eugene, Janice, Edward and Revell and his grandmother, Martha, for their love and support.

The author wishes to give special thanks to his Aunt Peggy Shinal Sims, who passed from this life in February 2021, and his mother, the late Mary E. "Honey" Humphrey, who passed from this life in October 2004.He knows that she is looking down on him and saying, "That's my George!"

ABSTRACT

This is not your ordinary book on management and managing people. At the beginning of the course that year, we were asked by the instructor to come up with our Biloxi Management Pearls (L269 Managing FEMA Staff on Disaster Operations). These are words of wisdom that we used or have used to guide each of us or me in my daily management of life and people.

The quotes or sayings in this book may not be perfect quotes, but more as we remember them. Some are quotes or sayings from family members, famous people, not-so-famous people, cartoons, books, and/or television shows. Some may even be from cartoon scripts, which we internalized and used as guiding principles for ourselves.

This book just goes to show that your inspiration can come from anywhere or anything, more particularly anyone. I hope you enjoy reading this book and my notes on what it means to me and the enjoyment I had in writing it.

The purpose of this book is to give the reader an insight into what makes managers and non-managers think. What helps guide our actions and or inaction when dealing with people and circumstances that we face? We truly are a product of our environment. Yes, I know, taken from Batman along with "This Town Needs an Enema".

Happy Reading!

Biloxi Management Pearl: When the only thing you have in your arsenal is a hammer, all problems look like nails.

Scripture: "If any of you lacks wisdom, you should ask God, who gives generously to all without finding fault, and it will be given to you." (James 1:5)

Application of Biloxi Management Pearl to the Lesson:

Personal Observation:

What are your leadership skills? How do you lead and manage people? If you do not possess such skills or you have limited skills, this is probably you. Ah, yes, this is the one-size fit all in leadership and management. It will work well when it comes to some clothing and headgear (hats); however, it is terrible for the management of people. If directing and telling people is all you have in your arsenal or what to do as a supervisor, then you will be directing and telling everyone what to-do. If all you know is to micromanage or directing, then that is what you will always be.

According to Situational Leadership Styles, there are four: Telling or Directing; Selling or Coaching; Participating or Supporting and Delegating. Directing according to the Situational leadership style, the leader or supervisor makes decisions surrounding the completion of the project. In addition to this, the supervisor also tasks the team members and provides them with the benefit of his/her experience in that regard.

It is a great tool for those who are new to the organization and those who do not know what to do. They will see you as a great supervisor/leader. The question is, what does it do for those who need coaching and/or delegation?

Coaching, on the other hand, refers to the style where the leader still maintains decisions, going forward, regarding what the employees' should be doing, as well as how and when it should be done. However, here, the supervisor affords opportunities for feedback from the employees.

Basically, the employer/team member who has the skill set and is just not sure of him/herself may become a bit annoyed. All they need is a little nudge or an ("Atta boy/girl" and some assurance. They do not need to be micromanaged or led to believe that they are being micromanaged. Eventually, directing this type of employee will lead to a breakdown in communication.

Delegating, according to the Situational leadership style, the leader or supervisor takes a back seat to the task at hand. Here, the leader has confidence in his/her employees or team members and better yet, the team members have confidence, and they are motivated that they can accomplish the task at an acceptable level with minimal supervision, if any at all.

Delegating is terrible for this type of person. He/she has the skill set and knows what needs to be done, how it should be done and sometimes, the timeline of when to do it and when it should be completed.

Now, the last to be mentioned is Participating leadership style. Here, the employee has the skills to perform the assigned task at hand at an acceptable level but lacks either the confidence or the motivation/commitment to do so.

As I have said all along, or tell people about myself, especially in my older years as a more seasoned employee/supervisor. "I am just like that old attack dog; just point me in the right direction and say, sic em." Why, you ask, because I do not lack the skills or the confidence (well, maybe the motivation, sometimes, depending on what the assignment is and how I feel, but that is another story). Using your only tool on this type of person will have him or her running for the hills or leaving the organization, so to speak, if they are being directed or micromanaged. They will eventually feel that they are not trusted or valued; in some cases, they may even feel that they are not respected or that you do not respect them or their skill set and abilities. Eventually, morale will be at an all-time low in the organization.

I remember when I was fresh out of college and became a supervisor for the first time. I was given one of the most difficult buildings with the most difficult employees. At the time, the only tool in my arsenal was Directing. Starting off, I was directing, and

I never let off. If they did not do the work as assigned, they were written up and eventually terminated. At one point, I was known as the Terminator (The movies had just come out around that time). However, as I told them, I did not terminate anyone; they terminated themselves. Yes, I was a hard-nosed, no-nonsense supervisor. Those I supervised were a lot older than me and tried to take advantage of my inexperience as a supervisor. Whenever a building or employees were having problems, I was moved to that building temporarily to get it back in shape, so to speak. I remember thinking back then, in management, it is a lot easier to start off hard and directing and then get easy than it is to start easy and try to get hard. I never took the time to get to know the people I supervised; it was work, plain and simple. After about two years, I had burned myself out. I believe the one tool in my arsenal had a lot to do with it.

I thank God that as the years went by, I added tools to my arsenal. I thank God because he allowed and showed me how to hone and perfect my craft. He showed me and allowed me to see the human side of the people I talked to. I started to understand life. I started to talk less and listen more. I started to seek to understand and then be understood. I started to use more laughter. I started to understand those words I had heard so long ago in two different ways.

1. Rule number 1 is don't sweat the small stuff.

And rule number 2 is everything is small stuff.

Or

2. Rule number 1 is don't sweat the small stuff.

Rule number 2 is see rule number 1.

In my later years as part of management, I had an employee tell me what I should be doing and that I was too hard and was hard headed. My reply was, "If I listen to what everyone told me, then they would be supervising me instead of the other way around." Also, if I was called in for making a bad decision, I can justify my own bad decision; I cannot justify someone else's bad decision. Last point, I remember asking one of my team members, just tell me the truth. If I allowed you to tell me what to do, you would not stop, nor would you listen to me going forward. Just be honest and tell me the truth. After a while, she thought about it, and she answered, yes, you are right. "That is my point".

I always told them that I must make the decisions that are best for the department/organization as a whole, not just what suits my fancy. In essence, I had stocked my arsenal, I was no longer one dimensional. In the process, and in addition to other things, I had discovered Integrity, humility, and compassion.

Build your arsenal, sharpen and maintain the tools in your arsenal. Know how, when and where to use each tool.

Thank you, Jesus; thank you, Lord!

Ethical Leadership Principles Found in the Bible

(Micah 6:8), *"He hath shewed thee, O man, what is good; and what doth the Lord require of thee, but to do justly, and to love mercy, and to walk humbly with thy God?"*

Integrity: Integrity is the bedrock of ethical leadership. Just as **(Proverbs 11:3)** warns, *"The integrity of the upright shall guide them: but the perverseness of transgressors shall destroy them,"* Leaders who consistently adhere to moral and ethical principles cultivate a thriving environment. Their honesty, transparency, and trustworthiness become the magnetic pull that attracts respect and loyalty from those they lead.

Because of honesty, there are a great many advantages brought about. It is easier for people to trust one another when the leader places a priority on ethical behavior. When people have faith in the individual who is heading in the right direction, they are more willing to put their energy and creativity into the endeavor. Because of this, an environment that encourages collaboration, productivity and open communication is created. The making of ethical decisions becomes a natural consequence because of this. When confronted with difficult decisions, leaders who are led by integrity are able to make judgments that are clear-headed and founded on the values they have established. Despite the fact that these decisions may not always be the simplest, they put the organization's long-term viability and good practices at the forefront of their priorities.

In addition, leaders who possess integrity become guiding lights of ethical behavior, which empowers people who are in their immediate vicinity. The activities that they take serve as a powerful example, motivating people to behave in a manner that is honest and has a significant moral compass. Because of this, a ripple effect is created, which helps to cultivate a healthy and ethical work culture in which everyone feels empowered to act in a manner that is appropriate.

There are obstacles to overcome on the route that leads to honesty. There is a constant strain on leaders to achieve greatness, and this pressure may occasionally entice them to take shortcuts or lower their standards. Avoiding this impulse is of the utmost importance. Leaders who possess integrity are immovable in their commitment to ethical behavior, placing it ahead of short-term rewards. Furthermore, there are occasions when there are no right or wrong responses to ethical conundrums. Under these circumstances, having a solid moral foundation becomes very necessary. Leaders who carry themselves with integrity are able to manage difficult circumstances by relying upon their fundamental principles in order to arrive at reasonable decisions.

Compassion: One of the most important skills that a leader may possess is compassion, which can be defined as the ability to comprehend and empathize with the feelings of other people. Compassion is cultivated by effective leaders in the same manner that Jesus showed it throughout his life by extending love and mercy to those who were on the margins of society. The manner in which they interact demonstrates the compassion that they possess. The people that the leader is leading are able to freely share their issues and frustrations because they become attentive listeners and provide a secure atmosphere for them to do so. By actively listening to their workers, leaders are able to create trust and understanding in the people. In addition to just listening, this compassion goes beyond that. Because of this, leaders are compelled to provide support and encouragement. They are aware of the issues that the people around them are experiencing and are actively looking for solutions to assist them in overcoming those obstacles. The provision of flexible work arrangements for those who are experiencing personal challenges, the provision of mentoring for the sake of professional development, or the simple delivery of a kind word at a stressful moment are all examples of what this may entail.

The impact of compassion goes beyond individual interactions. This helps to cultivate a culture of empathy and inclusion among the people. Through the demonstration of compassion, leaders are able to create an atmosphere in which all individuals, regardless of their background or experience, are made to feel appreciated and respected. This feeling of belonging gives people the confidence to take chances, communicate their ideas in an open manner, and work together in an efficient manner.

Justice: Justice, the absolute commitment to fairness and upholding moral principles, is a cornerstone of ethical leadership. The prophet Isaiah, in **(Isaiah 1:17)**, says, *"Learn to do well; seek judgment, relieve the oppressed, judge the fatherless, plead for the widow."* Ethical leaders heed this call, actively promoting equality and fairness among people.

This dedication to justice is shown in a number of different ways. One of the goals of ethical leaders is to arrive at judgments that are free from bias and prejudice. They make certain that everyone, regardless of their origin or affiliation, is provided with equal opportunity to participate and progress in their careers. When they are confronted with circumstances that may include misconduct, they respond to them in a prompt and equitable manner, so guaranteeing that everyone is held accountable.

Moreover, ethical leaders serve as champions for those who would not otherwise have a voice in the matter. They make sure that everyone feels comfortable enough to speak out and denounce abuses, and they advocate for the concerns of those who are historically oppressed. A culture of trust and psychological safety is established as a result of this, in which people are given the confidence to voice their concerns without the fear of being punished.

Humility: (Micah 6:8) offers a powerful reminder: *"He hath shewed thee, O man, what is good; and what doth the Lord require of thee, but to do justly, and to love mercy, and to walk humbly with thy God?"* Humility, the act of acknowledging one's limitations and seeking guidance beyond oneself, is a cornerstone of ethical leadership. Leaders who embody this quality understand they don't have all the answers. They are open to learning from others, drawing wisdom from diverse perspectives and experiences.

This humility is evident in several significant ways. Initially, it enables leaders to acknowledge their own shortcomings. They possess the humility to acknowledge their lack of expertise in all areas and are at ease soliciting advice from individuals who possess specialized knowledge or experience. This cultivates a cooperative atmosphere in which each individual is esteemed for their distinct contributions.

The second point is that humble leaders put the greater good ahead of their own selfish ambitions. The urge for self-aggrandizement is not the driving force behind their actions; rather, it is the desire to serve. And the organization is guiding them. When a follower realizes that his leader is sincerely concerned about his success, it develops trust and loyalty in him.

In the third place, humility opens the doors to criticism that is constructive. Feedback is not seen as a personal assault by humble leaders; rather, they see it as a chance for personal development. They make it a point to aggressively seek input from the people and are open to understanding diverse points of view. This helps to create an environment that values ongoing education and progress.

Leadership that exemplifies honesty, empathy, fairness, and humility provides an environment where people feel safe to share ideas and function together. They motivate the people around them to give their all-in pursuit of common objectives and help each individual realize his or her greatest potential. At the end of the day, society reaps the rewards of ethical leadership that is based on principles.

Biloxi Management Pearl: I don't believe in making your problem my problem

Scripture: *"These things I have spoken to you, so that in Me you may have peace. In the world, you have tribulation, but take courage; I have overcome the world." (John 16:33)*

Application of Biloxi Management Pearl to the Lesson:

Personal Observation:

Whose problem is it anyway? As a society, people do not mind relieving you of your money and giving you their problems, if you will take them. Life has taught me many things over the course of my six decades here on this earth. Like this one, of course, and another one is to pick it up, put it down, and leave it alone. Remember, if you don't have time to do it right the first time, where will you find time to do it over?

Here, you pick it up, the task, the assignment, etc., and you do not do your best. If you do or give it your best, then you put it down or pass it on. You have done your best, with no shortcuts, etc.

Now and then, you want to leave it alone. Sometimes, we overthink or overanalyze a problem. There comes a point when you must leave it alone. Trust God that you have done your best; if you did indeed, do your very best.

Now, as I stated earlier, I don't believe in making your problem my problem. As a young supervisor manager, I believe it was my duty and responsibility to solve all the ills of the world. They brought me a problem and I thought it was up to me to solve it. That is what I did; I had to fix it.

Fixing the problem, I was reading a book on leadership and management, or maybe it was an article, I really don't remember which. However, what I do remember is the author stating that if you have a problem and take it to your supervisor/manager, also take a solution to the problem. Why? It does a few things when you do, - It shows your supervisor that you are a forward thinker and that you, too, can solve a problem. 2nd, it demonstrates that you are aware of his/her other duties and responsibilities and, of course, tasks at hand, not that you are not important. However, his/hers is just more pressing. 3rd and final one is that that is why you were hired because he/she believes in you and your skill sets and abilities.

Remember now, when you come up with a problem and with your own solution, you are really asking for permission to use it and not for him/her to solve it. Also, since you are closer to the problem, you may have a better idea about the solution. Keep in mind the supervisor's manager can agree with you, or it will help focus his or her answer to be more in line with the organization.

As I became an older more seasoned supervisor manager, I began to realize that this is the way that it should be. The old way of talking to your supervisor about your problems and or concerns and waiting for a reply. Don't get me wrong, there are some things that the supervisor must answer and others that must be taken up the chain, especially when it involves policies and procedures, etc. In my later years as a supervisor, I started telling my team members, I am not going to make your problem my problem, and my suggestion is that you do the same.

I remember as we talked about these grants that we were working on, they would say well, the grant's recipient said that their Board would not let them do this, or their Board does not understand; what should I do? We really need this grant; what can I do? What should I tell my supervisor about this? I would look at my team members and say or repeat that I am sorry, but in accordance with policy, regulations, etc., this is what I can or cannot do. Keep repeating it; they will get the message sooner or later. Another one is who I need to talk to or who my board should call and talk to. My reply was always the same: who they must talk to and what they have to say to their Board is their problem, not yours. "Now, if you want to take ownership of their problem and help themselves with their problem, that is up to you. If you want to take on that responsibility, go right ahead". However, remember I can truthfully tell you that whatever you say outside of regulation and policies and procedures, I cannot protect you." Remember my saying, I am not going to make your problem my problem, and if I were you, I would advise you to do the same. If you give them a solution and it fails or turns out the wrong way, you will hear about it again, and then it really will be your problem.

I sometimes find myself reflecting or a self-assessment, if you will, on my life's journey thus far. Thinking about things such as my faith, motivation, boundaries, and its impact on my life overall. Take time out of your busy schedule and see where you are in your life's journey.

Just Saying.

Reflection Questions

Self-Assessment: In your personal and professional life, how do you now deal with the challenges and obligations that you face? When you find yourself taking on the troubles of others without any justification, do you find yourself doing so? Take some time to think about how you often react when faced with obstacles and problems.

Awareness of Boundaries: Are you able to identify situations in which you are being forced to deal with the issues of another person? Which of the following are some symptoms or clues that you could be taking on an excessive amount of responsibility for the problems of other people? Think of moments when you felt that you were being weighed down or overwhelmed by the issues of another person.

Understanding Motivations: For what reason do you feel driven to take on the troubles of other people? Do you have any underlying reasons, such as a need for control, a fear of disagreement, or a desire to satisfy other people? Give some thought to the ways in which these sources of motivation impact your actions and the decisions you make.

Setting Boundaries: To what extent do you now use tactics that allow you to establish limits and safeguard your personal well-being? When it comes to saying "no" or delegating work to other people, are there aspects of your life in which you might act with greater confidence? When establishing and maintaining appropriate boundaries, it is important to think about the practical measures you may take.

Faith Perspective: Your attitude to problem-solving and taking on the challenges of others is influenced by your belief system in what ways? When it comes to dealing with obstacles, you should think about how the concepts of trust, surrender, and dependence on God will affect your viewpoint.

Application in Relationships: What are some ways that you might convey the idea that you should not take on the issues of others to the people in your immediate environment, such as members of your family, friends, or coworkers? Consider the ways in which you might make your limits known in a manner that is courteous while yet providing support and encouragement to other people.

Long-Term Impact: What are the probable repercussions of accepting responsibility for the issues of others on a continuous basis? Take into consideration the influence on your own mental and emotional well-being, as well as the dynamics of your relationships and the duties you have under your account. When you think about how adopting a healthy approach to problem-solving may lead to better satisfaction and effectiveness in the long term, you should consider the following.

Engaging in analysis to respond to these reflection questions has the potential to significantly alter your approach to helping others. They help you examine your own inclinations: do you possess the qualities of a superhero who rushes to resolve issues, or do you prefer to delegate and provide support? Understanding one's patterns is an initial stride toward developing a more harmonious approach to helping others. Further, these questions encourage you to contemplate long-lasting results. Constantly assuming the burdens of others can deplete one's energy and place stress on interpersonal connections. Through thoughtful consideration of these potential repercussions, one can make decisions that nurture individual well-being and establish deeper interpersonal bonds.

Biloxi Management Pearl: Be consistently right or consistently wrong, but at least be consistent.

Scripture: "Therefore, my beloved brethren, be ye steadfast, unmoveable, always abounding in the work of the Lord, forasmuch as ye know that your labor is not in vain in the Lord."

(1 Corinthians 15:58)

Application of Biloxi Management Pearl to the Lesson:

Personal Observation

Merriam-Webster states that the word consistent is taken from the Latin word "*consistent-, consistent,* present participle of *consistent* "to come to a halt, remain at the same level, take up a position, reside, be composed of, be established." Basically, it is that of acting or doing something in the same way over and over again, a pattern or routine, if you will.

Consistency allows people to predict to a certain degree what their next action will be. Be mindful that we, as humans, are creatures of habit. If a person is consistent, it is easier to correct the mistake. Determine where the mistake was made, correct it, and it's all done. The problem develops when there is inconsistency. It is very difficult to find the problem because one cannot find out where the problem first occurred or if it occurred multiple times.

An inconsistent supervisor is terrible. I once had a supervisor/manager who was all over the place. One day, he/she is up, and the next day down. He/she was constantly changing his mind, depending on what day and time of day it was and who had told him what. For me, this was a horrible experience and a terrible place to work; one thing that was consistent about him/her is that he was inconsistent. Basically, or simply put, he/she was consistently inconsistent.

Morale was low, turnover was high, and there was no relief in sight. Many days, I prayed and said it's got to be a better way to make a living.

As I looked back at those times, it made me realize the type of leader/supervisor/manager that I did not want to be. I realized that I had to go through this to grow and get closer to God and allow him to guide me. Many of my sayings, philosophies and outlook on life and work were born here at this one job. One is that I believe that work should be fun, and I am going to do my best to keep it that way.

In adulthood, we spend most of our days getting ready for work, going to work, leaving work (commuting, before COVID anyway) talking about work. So, if it is that time-consuming of our lives, and it consumes most of our lives, not to mention hours in a day, should it not be fun? Your supervisor/manager can make it a good day, bad day or mediocre day. He/she can have a happy, sad, fun, or annoying day. I choose to make it a happy, fun day. If you see yourself anywhere except on that good or fun day, in the words/lyrics of the late great Michael Jackson, in the song Man in the Mirror, "… take a look at yourself and make that change".

Biloxi Management Pearl: a Great Team, is nothing more than a wise leader with committed followers.

Scripture: "Let nothing be done through selfish ambition or conceit, but in lowliness of mind let each esteem others better than himself. Let each of you look out not only for his own interests but also for the interests of others." **(Philippians 2:3-4)**

Application of Biloxi Management Pearl to the Lesson:

Personal Observation:

The only thing better than being a member or leader of a good team is being a member or being leader of a Great Team!! A team where everyone knows their role plays their role, but when something happens, as it will, they come together and pick up the slack when one of the teammates is out sick, without being told, in some cases.

If you look back at any great team, be it sports, company, organization, or business. What you will see at the core is a wise leader with committed followers. Think owners, CEOs, Head coaches, and the like. The leader should be wise enough to know and to select their team, if you will. If he does not pick his own team, he has those who are there who are committed followers in that they embody his vision as to what he/she wants.

His team sees and understands his vision and, in the same process, is committed to his vision. Now, let us examine and not get confused. The leader can come and go, and the followers will remain if the vision remains the same.

Have you ever wondered why organizations have vision statements and the like? It is to let everyone who comes there know what is expected of them. Now, again, this is not to say if there is no turnover in leadership that the organization will not fail. Quite the contrary, the vision may be the same, but the roadmap or the process may be different.

Have you not worked or been part of an organization or team, if you will, and the leadership changed, and it felt that it no longer seemed to be quite the same. Sometimes, you continue to stay there long past your welcome.

Also, remember the further away or higher up the leadership chain was the lesser of an impact it had on you.

I remember the last leadership role I had; while I was there the top leadership positions changed 5-6 times in a seven-year span. Although, for the most part, my immediate supervisor did not change over the course of those years, each change gnawed at me and my very existence there. With each passing day, week, and month, it changed a little bit more. I liked the first administration; they were more people-oriented; when the head man came to your office and sat down and talked to you and had a conversation or just to ask a question showed that he wanted to hear everything straight from me. The other administrations were more of the chain of command type. The chief of staff asked the deputy director to ask the office director to ask me. I would, in turn, explain to the office director, who would convey it to the deputy director, who would communicate to the chief of staff, who would answer the initial question posed by the executive director. I never knew what answer the executive director received after going through all those levels. I would venture to say, it was not the answer I gave.

Being a wise leader, I remember telling my team if you are right, I will be there for you. My team members respected me, and I, in turn, respected them. I try to live my mantra: "I believe work should be fun, and I am going to do my best to keep it that way.

I had my work, and they had their work. We joked and laughed, but we got our work done. When I needed something done at the last minute, yes, they grumbled, and yes, I knew, but they got me what I needed when I needed it on time, and it was correct. Although I COULD NOT GIVE RAISES ON THEIR BIRTHDAY EVERY YEAR, NOT ONLY DID I SEND THEM A BIRTHDAY EMAIL, FUNNY AND CORNY YES, BUT FOR SOME REASON THEY LIKED IT. IN ADDITION, I TOOK THEM OUT FOR A WORKING LUNCH, AS A GROUP OR A ONE-ON-ONE, WORKING LUNCH. This was done just to say, "I appreciate you and the work that you do." My core team never left the organization until I left for retirement. After I retired, they all left as well.

Now, on the flip side of the coin (at a different position at a different organization), my supervisor left about 3-5 months after he hired me. For the next year and a half, I was in complete and utter misery. The person who hired me and I, for the most part, were on the same wavelength; we communicated, and life was fun. After he left, things changed, and not for the better. I remember praying many days and nights saying, it's got to be a better way to make a living.

Yes, my prayers were answered. As the saying goes, He (God) may not come when you want him, but he will be there when you need him, or maybe He may not be there when you want him, but he is always right on time.

This reminds me of the quote from the movie Nancy McPhee: "When you need me, but do not want me, then I must stay. When you want me but no longer need me, then I have to go." Enough said.

Modern Day Examples:

The ideas of smart leadership and dedicated followership are more important than they have ever been in today's corporate climate, which is characterized by a fast-paced and sometimes turbulent environment. Companies such as Google and Amazon are successful because their CEOs are able to explain ideas that are crystal clear and cultivate cultures that encourage devotion and creativity among their workforce. Sundar Pichai, the Chief Executive Officer of Google, places a strong emphasis on fostering an environment that values innovation and ongoing education, and he encourages his staff to experiment and think creatively. This forward-thinking attitude has resulted in the development of ground-breaking products and services that have enabled Google to remain at the forefront of technological advancement.

Additionally, Jeff Bezos, the creator of Amazon, established the firm on the principles of putting the customer first, thinking about the long term, and being innovative. Bezos's leadership ideals, which include "Invent and Simplify" and "Hire and Develop the Best," have resulted in the establishment of an atmosphere in which people are given the authority to innovate and succeed in their work. The supremacy that Amazon has achieved in the fields of e-commerce and cloud computing may be attributed, in large part, to the company's dedication to a distinct vision and its cultivation of talent.

For both scenarios, it is essential for the leaders to be able to successfully convey their vision and create a workforce that is devoted to the organization. This strategy is not only responsible for the success of the firm, but it also provides adaptation and resilience in a market that is always shifting. These businesses are a shining example of the lasting significance of smart leadership and devoted followership because they create conditions that are conducive to the growth of creativity and dedication.

Scriptural Analysis:

(Philippians 2:3-4) encourages humility and selflessness, qualities essential for effective leadership. The scripture states,

"Do nothing out of selfish ambition or vain conceit. Rather, in humility, value others above yourselves, not looking to your own interests but each of you to the interests of the others." This was a call to unity and service within the setting of the early Christian church, which was essential for the development of a strong and cohesive community. It encouraged members to put aside their own goals and collaborate in a harmonic manner, creating an atmosphere in which the requirements of all individuals were taken into consideration and met. It is just as important for leaders to adhere to these values in order to ensure that they put the health and development of their teams ahead of their own personal goals in today's world. By exemplifying humility and selflessness, effective leaders are able to establish a culture that is characterized by trust and mutual respect. They generate loyalty and dedication from one another by recognizing the contributions of team members and concentrating on the objectives of the group as a whole. By using this strategy, people of the team are able to feel valued and driven to offer their best, which ultimately leads to increased morale and productivity.

Biloxi Management Pearl: "Different from, not better than – "Elizabeth's Momma"

Scripture: *"For there is no respect of persons with God."* ***(Romans 2:11, KJV).***

"For God does not show favoritism." ***(Romans 2:11, NIV).***

Application of Biloxi Management Pearl to the Lesson:

Personal Observation:

Different, Bing states that" is an adjective that means "not the same as another or each other" or "novel and unusual" or "distinct; unlike in nature, form, or quality." better, on the other hand, can also be an adjective that states a more excellent or effective type or quality. I must admit, I love Elizabeth's Mother saying. In management, we should be mindful that we are different, this is especially so in this world environment where we are all so diverse and bring different things to the table. Your viewpoint, outlook, and circumstances in life may be different from mine, but that does not make you or anyone else better than you. This goes for the President/ruler of a nation or CEO of an organization all the way down to the lowest person on the totem pole. We all have value, and we all have worth and something to contribute. Once we start looking at it from that vantage point, we will soon realize how great this world can be.

Remember, at least two things: one, when we look back on life, we realize that it was our family, church, and community (teachers, friends, etc.) that had the biggest impact on our lives, not CEOs and presidents. Secondly, the bible says that the poor will be with us always.

In this world in general and the United States, specifically, we should remember Elizabeth's Momma saying/quote. In the Black Lives Matter Movement, our black brothers and sisters are being killed and hurt at an alarming rate. Let us not forget our Asian brothers and sisters being beaten for no apparent reason other than the color of our skin, region, or ethnicity.

We are not better than them, and they are not better than us; we are all just different. For those of us who call ourselves Christians and those of us who do not see **(Romans 2:11)**, and if God does not, why should we? I am going to close and add a little something to the lyrics from O' Jays song Family Reunion.

It's a universal family. Under one divine purpose And one divine father That is, if we all come together no matter what color, race, or creed. Because that's all in the head whether you wanna believe it or not Cause' you'll bleed.

Cause you'll bleed. Yes, once you strip us of our outer covering (skin), you will realize we are all the same, a part of humans. So, in the grand scheme of things, the only thing that is different is the color of our skin. You know, skin, the largest organ of the body, with a total area of about 20 square feet. That layer of soft, elastic outer tissue covering the human body. Normally, it has three main functions: protection, regulation, and sensation. Unfortunately, some of us have decided to include a fourth function, to show how we are better than and not different from each other. It is interesting how much influence, power, weight that we as humans give to this organ.

Thank you, Elizabeth's mother, for putting it all in perspective: different from, not better than!!

Scriptural Insights

Throughout the Bible, there are several verses that emphasize the significance of equality and the one-of-a-kind worth that each and every person has. Here are some key scriptures that reinforce the principle of being different:

Galatians 3:28 (KJV) *states, "There is neither Jew nor Greek, there is neither bond nor free, there is neither male nor female: for ye are all one in Christ Jesus."*

This powerful verse emphasizes the unity and equality of all people in Christ, regardless of their background or social status. In the early Christian community, this declaration was revolutionary, as it challenged the deeply entrenched societal hierarchies and divisions of the time.

Paul was addressing the substantial ethnic and religious gap that existed between Jews and non-Jews when he made the proclamation that there was no distinction between Jews and Gentiles. This message was revolutionary because it extended an invitation to non-Jews to become part of the chosen people of God without mandating that they follow Jewish law. This was done in order to foster an inclusive environment. Equally transformational was the assertion that there is neither a slave nor a free person. This statement enhanced the status of slaves in a culture where slavery was a prevalent practice, and slaves were regarded as property. It acknowledged the intrinsic value of slaves and acknowledged their equality before God. It was an appeal to the Christian community to treat all people with dignity and respect, regardless of their socioeconomic status, and it was made without discrimination.

Similarly, Paul was fighting for gender equality when he said that there is no such thing as male or female. This was a strong statement of women's equal importance and participation in the Christian community, which was particularly significant in a culture that was characterized by patriarchy and in which women sometimes had restricted rights and were seen as subservient to males. The premise that despite the fact that we may be different from one another in a variety of ways, including socially, gender-wise, and ethnically, no one is necessarily superior to another is reaffirmed by this poem. The essential Christian premise that all Christians are equal and connected in Christ is emphasized by this aspect of the Christian faith. As we recognize that our differences do not lessen our common humanity and worth in the eyes of God, this message continues to be relevant in today's world, urging us to accept diversity and support equality in our communities. Our differences do not decrease our shared humanity.

James 2:1-4 (KJV) *states, "My brethren, have not the faith of our Lord Jesus Christ, the Lord of glory, with respect of persons. For if there come unto your assembly a man with a gold ring, in goodly apparel, and there come in also a poor man in vile raiment; And ye have respect to him that weareth the gay clothing, and say unto him, Sit thou here in a good place; and say to the poor, Stand thou there, or sit here under my footstool: Are ye not then partial in yourselves, and are become judges of evil thoughts?"*

Favoritism and prejudice based on outward looks or social standing are also things that are cautioned against in this verse. It addresses a problem that is prevalent in social and religious gatherings, which is that people may be assessed and treated differently depending on their income or external appearance. James draws attention to the superficial judgments that people often make by showing the situation of a wealthy man and a poor man attending a conference. He emphasizes the fact that people tend to give preferential treatment to those who look to be wealthy while marginalizing those who are less fortunate. The act of providing a comfortable seat for the wealthy individual while instructing the less fortunate one to either stand or sit on the floor indicates a profound prejudice that is in direct opposition to the teachings of Jesus Christ. Not only does this conduct discriminate against those who are less fortunate, but it also reflects the depraved ideas and unfair judgments that are prevalent among the community of believers. In contrast to the fundamental Christian teachings of love, equality, and respect for all people, regardless of their economic standing, this partiality is in direct opposition to these principles.

The advice expressed by James emphasizes the need to treat all individuals with equal respect and dignity, highlighting the fact that one's outer look should not be used to judge their value or the level of treatment one gets. It encourages believers to embody the values of fairness and impartiality by challenging them to reflect on their attitudes and behaviors and challenging them to acknowledge their own shortcomings. Through the rejection of favoritism, Christians are obligated to establish a society in which every individual is respected and acknowledged in an equal manner, therefore reflecting the all-encompassing love that Christ embodies. This message is still very important in today's culture because it encourages us to face and ultimately triumph over the prejudices that contribute to inequity and injustice.

<u>**1 Corinthians 12:12-27 (KJV)**</u> states, "For as the body is one, and hath many members, and all the members of that one body, being many, are one body: so also, is Christ. For by one Spirit are we all baptized into one body, whether we be Jews or Gentiles, whether we be bond or free; and have been all made to drink into one Spirit. For the body is not one member, but many. If the foot shall say, Because I am not the hand, I am not of the

body; is it therefore not of the body? And if the ear shall say, Because I am not the eye, I am not of the body; is it therefore not of the body? If the whole body were an eye, where was the hearing? If the whole were hearing, where were the smelling? But now hath God set the members every one of them in the body, as it hath pleased him. And if they were all one member, where was the body? But now there are many members, but one body. And the eye cannot say unto the hand, I have no need of thee: nor again the head to the feet, I have no need of you. Nay, much more those members of the body, which seem to be more feeble, are necessary: And those members of the body, which we think to be less honorable, upon these we bestow more abundant honor; and our uncomely parts have more abundant comeliness. For our comely parts have no need: but God hath tempered the body together, having given more abundant honor to that part which lacked. That there should be no schism in the body; but that the members should have the same care one for another. And whether one member suffers, all the members suffer with it; or if one member is honored, all the members rejoice with it. Now ye are the body of Christ, and members in particular."

By using the body as a metaphor, this compelling illustration demonstrates how every individual, with their own set of skills and functions, is equally important to the whole. The imagery of the human body is used by Paul to communicate the concept that, despite the fact that the body is one thing, it is composed of a great number of separate parts, each of which has a unique purpose. In the same way that a body cannot work correctly if it disregards the role that any of its components play, the community of believers, which is also referred to as the body of Christ, cannot function successfully if it does not acknowledge and value the contributions that each member makes.

The eye, the hand, the head, and the feet each represent distinct members of the community, each of whom plays an important function individually. Because each component is interrelated and reliant on the others, the eye cannot disregard the hand, and the brain cannot disregard the feet. Both of these components are interdependent. Because of this connection, the importance of variety within a community is brought to light. Every individual has a distinct set of abilities and points of view, both of which are essential for the overall health and functionality of the body.

The message of Paul encourages Christians to understand and accept their own duties as well as the roles of others, which helps to cultivate a culture of mutual respect and collaboration. It does this by highlighting the fact that all members of the community, regardless of the exact duties they do, are equally essential, which challenges any preconceptions of superiority or inferiority that occur within the community.

This idea continues to be applicable in the modern world, serving as a reminder that the variety of abilities, viewpoints, and contributions that exist within any organization, team, or community is what makes it possible for the group to achieve success. In the same way that a well-functioning body is able to achieve harmony and efficiency, we can accomplish a harmonious and successful operation by respecting and integrating the unique abilities of each individual member. The use of this metaphor highlights the significance of unity, variety, and interdependence. It encourages us to collaborate for the benefit of the community and acknowledges that every individual has something of value to give for the greater good.

Biloxi Management Pearl: There are 16 types of people in the world, but I cannot begin to know or understand them until I first know myself.

Scripture: *"For the Lord gives wisdom; from his mouth come knowledge and understanding...." **(Proverbs 2:6, NRSV).***

*"For the Lord giveth wisdom: out of his mouth cometh knowledge and understanding" **(Proverbs 2:6, KJV).***

Application of Biloxi Management Pearl to the Lesson:

Personal Observation:

Are there 16 types of people in the world? Maybe, maybe not. However, one can make the case that the author of this quote is referring to the Myers-Briggs type indication. According to the website, Personality typing is a system of categorizing people according to their tendencies to think and act in particular ways. The personality types, as proposed by Myers and Briggs, are that there were four key dimensions that could be used to categorize people. These four include Introversion vs. Extraversion, Sensing vs. Intuition, Thinking vs. Feeling and Judging vs. Perceiving. Each of the four dimensions is a choice between one and the other or your preferred style on each of the four dimensions. The sum of a person's four preferred styles becomes their personality type.

There are a total of 16 personality types. Eight are introverted tendencies or those people who are energized by spending quiet time alone or with a small group. They tend to be more reserved and thoughtful. While the others are more extroverted or those who are energized by spending time with people and in busy, active surroundings. They tend to be more expressive and outspoken.

So, based on this, there very well may be 16 types of people. I really don't know, but I do know that you must first know yourself. Knowing oneself is the epitome of self-actualization and realizing who and what you are and how you are energized. The question to ask yourself is, do you really know yourself? Some people go through their whole lives and can't answer this question. Others are married to the same person or have known the person most of their lives and still do not know the person.

You hear some people tell others that if this happened to me, I would do this, or I would do that. Well, maybe, but we all make decisions that we believe to be right and that is best at that point and time. We sometimes find ourselves asking the question, why in the world did I do that, or why did I go there? What was I thinking back then?

This is not to say that you cannot first know yourself, really, it is just the opposite. You can get to know yourself once you take the time to realize that as you grow older and that as you learn better you do better. Basically, let the word of God or pray and ask the will of God to guide you. At this point, you no longer must worry about the 16 other types, but the one that matters that will help and guide you to know yourself. It all begins with knowing who you are and whose you are.

I have taken the Myer Briggs twice, once in my early years of work and again in my later years. In my early years, I was told that they (the test giver) had never seen anyone like me before. A person who had no predominant way of doing things, about as close to the middle or as even as could be.

Talking to the tester, I remember telling the tester that I was a true introvert; however, I have siblings who are true extroverts, so I became a learned extrovert. To hang with them, I had to learn to think and act like them. Don't get me wrong, it tired me out, but I was able to hang with the "Big Dogs." Later in life, when I took it again, my personality became that of my true nature.

It is difficult, if not impossible, to successfully manage or lead others until you first know yourself. Again, take time out of your busy schedule and see where you are in your life's journey, as it relates to knowing thyself. Some of us will go through most, if not our entire lives and not know who we are. Others have been or are married and do not know their spouse or significant others. Take a few minutes and read and reflect to realize who you are and whose you are.

Proverbs 4:7 (KJV)

"Wisdom is the principal thing; therefore, get wisdom: and with all thy getting get understanding."

When it comes to knowing oneself, seeking knowledge and insight is not only essential but also forms the foundation of both personal and leadership greatness. The process of acquiring wisdom begins with developing an awareness of oneself. Wisdom is not only the acquisition of information; rather, it is the prudent use of that knowledge. Individuals are able to obtain a clearer perspective on their behaviors and choices when they engage in self-reflection and strive to develop better awareness of their own values, motivations, strengths, and flaws. This self-awareness helps cultivate humility and empathy, two qualities that are essential for effective leadership. Having the capacity to connect with other people and to make judgments that are both informed and fair is essential to effective leadership. When it comes to recognizing their own biases, managing their emotions, and maintaining their integrity, leaders who have a greater understanding of themselves are more suited. This kind of self-awareness makes it easier to have genuine interactions with others and instills trust in both peers and subordinates.

Self-awareness is the foundation upon which personal development is built. It creates an environment that encourages ongoing learning and adaptation, which enables people to manage the challenges of life with resilience and grace. The cultivation of a mentality that is receptive to learning and progress may be accomplished by persons who own their limits and actively pursue advancement. The first step in gaining knowledge and comprehension is to get familiar with oneself. This self-knowledge is not a fixed condition but rather a dynamic and continual journey that strengthens one's potential for leadership and personal growth, eventually leading to a life that is more satisfying and has a greater effect.

Psalm 139:23-24 (KJV) *"Search me, O God, and know my heart: try me, and know my thoughts: And see if there be any wicked way in me, and lead me in the way everlasting."*

Individuals are encouraged to engage in self-examination and seek the direction of God in order to gain an awareness of their actual nature. By inviting God to examine your heart, you might achieve a remarkable level of self-awareness, uncovering reasons that you were previously unaware of, and providing direction toward personal development and integrity. You are able to accept a higher level of truth and reflection when you voluntarily expose yourself to the examination of the divine. Your self-deception or ignorance may have concealed some facets of your character, but this method will shed light on those qualities. The insight that God gives offers an objective viewpoint, which assists in identifying and addressing areas in which personal prejudices or weaknesses that are not seen by the individual impede progress. You are able to strive toward meaningful change and harmony with your fundamental ideas and values if you acknowledge these hidden qualities.

In addition, heavenly guidance provides both clarity and direction. The road of justice and honesty is fostered as a result of its ability to direct you away from behaviors and beliefs that might be harmful to your well-being and the connections you have. The values of honesty, humility, and compassion are reinforced by the cultivation of a more profound relationship with your religion via the establishment of this spiritual partnership. It takes a tremendous act of humility and openness to invite God to probe your heart. In essence, this is what invitation means. It gives you the opportunity to go on a path of self-discovery that strengthens your personal integrity and progress, bringing your life into closer alignment with divine knowledge and purpose. When this process is completed, the result is a life that is more genuine, purpose-driven, and founded on moral and spiritual clarity.

James 1:5 (KJV) *"If any of you lack wisdom, let him ask of God, that giveth to all men liberally, and upbraideth not; and it shall be given him."*

Knowing oneself is not just an intellectual pursuit but also a spiritual one. By asking God for wisdom, you acknowledge that true understanding of oneself comes from divine insight and guidance. Prayer becomes a vital tool in this process, serving as a means of communication with the divine and a source of spiritual illumination. Through prayer, you open your heart to God's presence, inviting His wisdom to penetrate the depths of your soul. This act of seeking divine insight fosters a deeper connection with your spiritual identity, allowing you to see beyond surface-level perceptions and understand the core of your being. It reveals hidden motivations, strengths, and weaknesses that might be overlooked through mere intellectual reflection.

Divine wisdom offers a perspective that transcends human limitations, providing clarity and truth that can guide your personal growth. It helps align your actions and decisions with your higher purpose and values, leading to a more fulfilling and meaningful life. By seeking God's wisdom, you embrace a holistic approach to self-discovery that integrates both mind and spirit. In essence, the journey of knowing oneself is enriched by the spiritual dimension of prayer and divine wisdom. It transforms self-discovery into a sacred quest for deeper understanding, aligning your inner life with divine purpose and insight. This spiritual approach to self-awareness ensures that your growth is grounded in truth and guided by higher wisdom.

Biloxi Management Pearl: "He who controls others is strong, He who controls himself is mighty." (Tarzan, animated version).

Scripture: *"It is better to be patient than powerful; it is better to have self-control than to conquer a city"* **(Proverbs 16:32)**, *New Living Translation (NLT))*.

Application of Biloxi Management Pearl to the Lesson:

Personal Observation:

Yes, this is one of mine. I remember this from when I was a child, looking at the animated Tarzan TV show, and back in the 1970s-80s. At the time that I heard it, I thought that it was so stirring and thought-provoking to my young mind. To this day, I still remember the impact it had on me, and it has guided me all these years to develop into the person that I am now.

The need to control others can be viewed as a vice or a flaw, if you will. We all have vices. Vice is defined as a bad or immoral behavior or habit, a moral flaw or weakness, or it could be a minor bad habit. Regardless of what it is, you must have self-control to help overcome it.

I have always had problems with my weight. Yes, I want to lose weight, but with any vice or habit, you must have self-control to do the things that you need to do. I did not, well not until the second semester of my senior year in high school.

As supervisors/managers, we either have (developed from our youth) or develop vices (during adulthood). As managers/supervisors, we should be constantly on guard for how these vices control us, our lives and those we supervise.

In management we are constantly adjusting ourselves and our temperament to the persons we supervise. Be it coaching, delegating, informing, supporting and or directing. Directing people what to do follows the rules and guidelines, but one must first look at themselves and within themselves and realize it is so easy to tell someone else what they should and ought to do and how hard it is to tell yourself what to do and then do it and stick with it. In essence, we must have faith in who we are, what we do and, most important, God.

If we think back and remember Luke 7, the centurion who wanted Jesus to heal his servant, he states that he tells people/soldiers to do this, and they do it; he tells them to go there, and they go there. But he realized the fact that Jesus need not come to his place, but just to say that his servant be healed, and he will be healed. Jesus noted the faith that the centurion had, and the servant was healed.

So, what good is it to control others, through force or psychologically, if you cannot control that impulse yourself? Remember, we are only as good as we allow ourselves to be. God gives us free will to do what we want, to serve him or not to serve him. To do right or to do wrong. If we seek his word and his guidance, yes, he will help us. However, we first must seek his help and guidance. We can only seek his help and guidance if we want it. Now, this is where "will power" and "self-control" comes in. Basically, you must want to have that self-control.

We all have vices; without self-control, you will be at the mercy of whatever vice you may have. Remember, we can do all things through Christ Jesus, who strengthens us. Keep this in mind when you are having problems when those impulses start to get too strong, and you feel that you must indulge. You feel that "will power" waning, and you start to move into desperation mode. If you believe and have faith, you will find yourself getting stronger. Now, if you are not sure on where to start, here is a verse that will get you moving in the right direction.

Galatians 5:22-23 (KJV)

"But the fruit of the Spirit is love, joy, peace, longsuffering, gentleness, goodness, faith, Meekness, temperance: against such there is no law."

This particular passage emphasizes the fact that self-control is a fruit that the Holy Spirit offers. For those in positions of authority and management, it implies that self-control is a divine characteristic that may be developed via spiritual development. Developing these attributes not only contributes to one's own personal development but also helps one become a more patient and compassionate leader who can successfully guide others. Self-control is essential in the context of management and leadership because it enables leaders to respond deliberately rather than reacting hastily to situations. A culture of respect and understanding is encouraged by this attribute, which contributes to the development of a tranquil and stable working environment. When leaders exhibit self-control, they set an example for their team members on how to behave, which in turn encourages them to behave with the same level of restraint and thoughtfulness, which ultimately leads to increased overall harmony and productivity.

Furthermore, the fact that self-control is a fruit of the Holy Spirit suggests that this quality is developed via one's connection with God and through continual spiritual growth. The acts of leaders who make an investment in their spiritual development are more likely to be led by higher principles and ideals, which increases the likelihood that they will consistently demonstrate self-control. This spiritual foundation has the potential to give the courage and insight that is required to manage difficult circumstances with grace and integrity. The development of self-control enables leaders to more successfully handle disputes, improve their decision-making abilities, and keep their calm even when they are under intense pressure. Not only does this improve their leadership qualities, but it also helps them develop trust and credibility with their team. Additionally, leading with patience and compassion, which are directly connected to self-control, generates a pleasant and supportive work environment in which workers feel appreciated and driven. This atmosphere is created by someone who is in a position of leadership.

Biloxi Management Pearl: Every time you walk past a mistake, you endorse it.

Scripture: *"I, therefore, the prisoner of the Lord, beseech you that ye walk worthy of the vocation wherewith ye are called."*
Ephesians 4:1 (KJV)

Application of Biloxi Management Pearl to the Lesson:

Personal Observation:

Two words here that we must first define: Mistake and Endorse. Merriam-Webster states that a Mistake means a wrong judgment or a wrong action or statement proceeding from faulty judgment, inadequate knowledge, or inattention. On the other hand, endorse means to approve openly or to recommend usually for financial compensation. So, here we see that if you see or hear something and we do not correct it, then we are indeed approving it and even maybe recommending it if money is involved.

Yes, this is correct. During this time of racial disparity and reckoning, to say I am not a racist is not good enough. If you see an act of racism going on and you do nothing, then in my mind, you are just as culpable. This is not to say that you are to put yourself in harm's way, but if it is your friends who are doing the deed, and you say nothing, then you agree with them and what they stand for.

Let us also include the word incorrect or something that is wrong. In management as well as in life, if you see something wrong and not say something you are indeed in approval of the deed, plain and simple. We should remember that God created us all, and to use a quote from our Sunday School Class, we are all God's creation, but we are not all his people. Remember, if you see a child being bullied, a minority being treated unfairly, or an employee doing something that they should not do, as management (and/or you have the ability), you are responsible for correcting it, and if you do not, by default, you are endorsing it or agreeing with it.

This brings an interesting point to mind. I had a team member who once asked me why I had to correct everything that I saw wrong with their work. My reply: 1. I had a supervisor who trusted me and my work, and when she signed off on it, she knew I would check it and review it thoroughly. Did she check my work? Yes, she did, but it was more of a spot check than a check to see if I had done my job. The other reason is that we, as humans, are bound to make mistakes because we are not perfect beings. So, if I turn a blind eye to something or a mistake that I do find, it will only compound the mistake. Basically, I am endorsing the mistake.

Endorsing a mistake will only lead to problems and more mistakes down the road. This includes your work, professional life as well as your personal and spiritual life. Remember, you are judged by the company that you keep, whether you believe it or not. Because it has been said, if a friend, coworker, supervisor, honestly loves, respects you, etc., he will not hesitate to correct you, if needed be (not in an embarrassing or demeaning way, of course). By that same token, a true friend, coworker, etc. will in turn thank him for his honesty and conduct himself according, going forward.

Proverbs 27:5 (KJV)

"Open rebuke is better than secret love!"

This verse emphasizes that sincere correction is more valuable than mute tolerance. It implies that it is more advantageous for leaders to openly and constructively acknowledge and rectify errors rather than disregard them. It is impossible to exaggerate the significance of candid correction in management and leadership. By openly acknowledging and rectifying errors, leaders foster an atmosphere characterized by transparency and responsibility. This strategy prevents minor issues from escalating into major complications by ensuring that employees are cognizant of the organization's standards and expectations. A culture of continuous improvement is fostered by constructive feedback, in which errors are regarded as chances for development and learning rather than as grounds for embarrassment or frustration.

Furthermore, real correction helps to cultivate trust and confidence among leaders and the people they supervise. The credibility and trustworthiness of a leader are bolstered when subordinates notice that the leader is willing to engage in uncomfortable debates and provide guidance. In order to ensure effective cooperation and collaboration, it is essential to cultivate trust since it encourages open communication and a willingness to share views and opinions. As an alternative, the practice of quiet tolerance may lead to a wide variety of issues. When faults in performance criteria are ignored or overlooked, it is possible for there to be inconsistency and confusion as a consequence. It is possible that employees who continue to make the same mistakes may be unaware of their faults, which can have a detrimental effect on the morale and energy of the team. Furthermore, the absence of obvious repercussions may lead to a lack of accountability among workers, who may be deterred from accepting responsibility for their behavior as they are not able to see the consequences of their actions.

Biloxi Management Pearl: If you don't start any crap, there won't be any crap.

Scripture: "And the work of righteousness shall be peace, and the effect of righteousness quietness and assurance forever."
(Isaiah 32:17) (KJV)

Application of Biloxi Management Pearl to the Lesson:

Personal Observation:

This is an oldie and a goodie. According to the Oxford Language Dictionary, the term "crap" is defined as something of extremely poor quality or excrement. Let us focus on extremely poor quality. As supervisors/managers, this is what we will get from the people we supervise if we fail to do our part.

Please be cognizant that as a member of management, our ultimate responsibility is keeping the organization, shift, store or what have you running and operating in top condition. So, if we do not do our job to the utmost of our responsibility or if we dare allow the people we supervise to deviate from the norm or the policies and procedures as outlined in the employee's handbook, or if we fail to do our due diligence when problems arise, this is what we will end up with "crap".

Here, if you do not entertain extremely poor-quality work, there will not be any extremely poor-quality work.

Without poor-quality work, you will not have any problems, and that is a good thing. I had a saying that I used to tell the people I supervise, "If you do what you are supposed to do, I will not do what I have to do." Then, in essence, you will not be starting any crap, and you don't expect them to start any crap; therefore, there will not be any crap on your end (write-up, disciplinary reports, etc.).

Now, take a moment and look back over your years of work and see if you don't see this somewhere. It does not have to be in your work life, it may be in your personal life or social life. One example is that people will talk to everyone the same way or treat everyone the same way because that is all they have in their arsenal. Remember, "You play too much" or "Do you ever take anything seriously?" Sometimes, it is a coping mechanism, and sometimes, that is all they had in their arsenal at the time.

I will close this pearl out with a point or two: whether we see ourselves as Christians or not, we must learn (**L**ook to **E**stablish **A**ctual **R**equired **N**eeds) to expand and enlarge our arsenal so we can meet people where they are. We cannot help or understand their needs until we can do that. Keep in mind that during Jesus' Ministry here on earth and while recruiting his disciples, he met them where they were, and even today, he meets us where we are.

The second point I want to make comes from an old Chinese proverb, I think, and it goes something like this.

He who knows and knows not that he knows is asleep, awaken him.

He who knows and knows that he knows is a wise man; follow him.

He who knows not and knows not that he knows not is a fool; shun him.

Biloxi Management Pearl: Blessed are we who are flexible because we rarely get bent out of shape.

*Scripture: "Trust in the Lord with all your heart and lean not on your own understanding; In all your ways acknowledge Him, And He shall direct your paths." **(Proverbs 3:5-6 (NKJ).***

: "Yet, O Lord, you are our Father; we are the clay, and you are our potter; we are all the work of your hand" (Isaiah 64:8, NRSV).

"But now, O Lord, thou art our father; we are the clay, and thou, our potter; and we all are the work of thy hand" (Isaiah 64:8, KJV).

Application of Biloxi Management Pearl to the Lesson

Personal Observation:

Merriam states that flexibility is characterized by a ready capability to adapt to new, different, or changing requirements.

When we are flexible, it is true that we cannot or rarely get bent out of shape. We take what is given and make the best of it. Be it a supervisor, upper-level supervisor/manager who tells a middle or lower-level supervisor how he/or she wants something done. We do not get upset or disappointed; we do what is asked and required, within reason, of course.

However, if we are open and flexible, then we will have no preconceived ideas or notions, and we are open to accepting the perfect will of God. I remember, doing our Sunday School Lesson the question was asked in what ways openness and a listening ear can provide opportunities. The reply, you ask, "We must be attentive and respond to the Gospel message with faithfulness and generous hospitality."

FEMA flexible is the term used early and often when I worked with FEMA during the relief of Hurricane Katrina. During that time, we used it to keep us mentally alert or ready for any changes in policy that may come about. During that time, Katrina, as we now refer to it, was arguably the costliest storm, among other things, to make landfall in the United States. The size, wind span, storm surge, etc. Some will argue that it was the perfect storm. So, the "perfect storm" rewrote the emergency management policies that probably still exist as of this writing.

Because of these updates and changes, we had to be flexible. Flexible enough to start down one path, just to be told later that it can no longer be applied in this or that situation, if at all. We must be flexible enough to realize and understand that nothing in this world lasts forever. Maybe that is the way it was done last year or last month, for that matter, but that is not how it is done now. We learned to adapt or change on the fly. Survivors of this massive storm needed our help, and the current policy was not designed for times like these.

Those who could not adapt to new, different, or changing requirements left as it became too much. Others who could adapt to new, different, or changing requirements stayed. Why, you ask, because we were blessed and flexible and rarely got bent out of shape. We accepted the challenge and went toward it with the understanding that it might change before we got there. As for me personally, **Proverbs 3:5-6 (NKJ)**, what else can I say?

Biloxi Management Pearl: Knowledge is power. And knowledge is something no one can take away from you.

Scripture: "Wise warriors are mightier than strong ones, and those who have knowledge than those who have strength." (Proverbs 24:5, NRSV).

"A wise man is strong; yea, a man of knowledge increased strength." (Proverbs 24:5, KJV).

Application of Biloxi Management Pearl to the Lesson:

Personal Observation:

This is a very True statement: Knowledge is power, and it is something no one can take away from you other than God himself. A few things we must think about knowledge, as it is different from smartness and intelligence. Although they are sometimes used interchangeably, there is a difference. Smart is defined by Merriam as very good at learning or thinking about things or being intelligent or showing intelligence or good judgment or being wise.

Now, the definition of **Intelligence** is the ability to gather knowledge and skills and apply them to your life.

Knowledge, according to Merriam, is the fact or condition of knowing something with familiarity gained through experience or association

(2): acquaintance with or understanding of a science, art, or technique

b (1): the fact or condition of being aware of something

(2): the range of one's information or understanding; the circumstance or condition of apprehending truth or fact through reasoning: Cognition or the sum of what is known: the body of truth, information, and principles acquired by humankind. So, if this is the case, smartness is the ability to learn or think about things individually whereas knowledge is the full range of an individual's information or understanding of apprehending the truth or facts. Therefore, intelligence is the ability or culmination of this knowledge and or skills and applying them to your everyday life. In essence, that knowledge becomes part of who you are, or your personality, the set of emotional qualities and or behavior that makes us what and who we are and those qualities that make each of us as persons different from other people in this world, our uniqueness.

Knowledge is the sum of who we are and what we will become based on our life experiences and education (formal & informal), and that is power. However, also, bear in mind although knowledge is power it is about how you use that power. If you use it wisely to build others up, that is good; however, if you use it to belittle or to make others feel inferior, then you are using it the wrong way. This goes back to "Different from, not better than." The knowledge and power make you different from, not better than, others around you; use it wisely.

Knowledge is power in that it can and will take you to many places and will allow you to do many things. Use it wisely and remember that God and our Lord and Savior Jesus have all the power in Heaven and Earth. Any knowledge or power that he bestows upon us should be used to lift his kingdom and treat our fellow man and woman with the love and respect that he desires.

Use your God-given gifts wisely.

James 1:5 (KJV):

"If any of you lack wisdom, let him ask of God, that giveth to all men liberally, and upbraideth not; and it shall be given him."

This passage emphasizes the importance of seeking knowledge from God and emphasizes that spiritual guidance is easily accessible to those who take the time to inquire about it. This demonstrates the significance of having a humble attitude and being prepared to accept assistance in order to acquire information. The relevance of this passage lies in the fact that it emphasizes the need to acknowledge one's own limits and the requirement for direction from other sources, especially from a higher and more heavenly source. It is essential for persons in leadership positions or in any other capacity to recognize that they do not possess all of the answers in order to make good decisions and to further their own personal development. This practice of seeking wisdom is not just about acquiring information; it is also about developing a more profound feeling of humility and reliance on God.

The process is greatly aided by the presence of humility. It is a sign of a humble spirit to acknowledge that one is in need of assistance and to pray to God for guidance. This humility is a crucial virtue, particularly for those who hold leadership positions, since it helps to create an atmosphere in which learning and development are emphasized. Leaders who exhibit humility are more accessible and open to criticism, which helps to establish a culture in which members of the team feel appreciated and are encouraged to offer their thoughts and opinions. The desire to seek assistance and direction is absolutely necessary in order to acquire genuine information and comprehension. When people pray to God for knowledge, they are allowing themselves to be exposed to thoughts and viewpoints that are beyond the comprehension of human beings. The capacity to manage complicated circumstances with discernment and grace may be gained via the use of this divine knowledge, which can bring clarity and guidance.

It is possible for leaders to improve their decision-making processes by seeking knowledge from God, which in turn enables them to lead with more confidence and integrity. It provides them with the understanding that is necessary to successfully handle problems, manage disagreements, and motivate their teams. This dependence on divine direction may also foster a feeling of serenity and certainty in the individual, as they are aware that they are not alone in their obligations and that they have access to an unlimited reservoir of understanding.

Biloxi Management Pearl: "Man is the principal syllable in management." C.T. McKenzie

Scripture: "Blessed are you, O land, whose king is of nobility and whose princes eat at the appropriate time–for strength and not for drunkenness." (Ecclesiastes 10:17)

Application of Biloxi Management Pearl to the Lesson:

Personal Observation:

Man is the principal syllable in management. It is all about how you treat your fellow man. Being fair and honest, not using stereotypes, and accepting those who may not look, talk or act like you. So, the basic question here is, what kind of manager or supervisor are you? Are you a stress reducer or a stress producer for your team members? Now, think about that question in two ways: how do you see yourself, and how do your team members see you?

Are you or do you consider yourself as being fair, reasonable, and/or appreciative? Put another way, do you lead by example, provide clear direction, share credit for accomplishments and appreciate others?

Are you consistent, calm under pressure, smart/intelligent, knowledgeable, even-tempered with an easy going/good sense of humor?

Do you give employees self-worth by welcoming opinions that are different from your own? Are you supportive and allow mistakes/accountability and sincerity when open to suggestions?

If the answer is yes, then you are viewed as a manager as stress reducers. Your team trusts you and will do everything they can for you. They will follow you.

Now, on the other hand, are you just the opposite? Do you see yourself, or do your team members see you as a whip, moody, micromanaging, commanding, demanding, power-tripping hypocrite? Are you viewed as being inconsistent when tasking your team, or maybe tasking them without discussion? How are your communication skills? Are they good or poor? Do you or have you managed with negative emotions (anger, criticism)? What about respect? Do you lack respect or fail to acknowledge the achievements of others on your team?

When setting goals and deadlines, are they realistic and achievable? Do others see you as knowing your job, as providing positive feedback, and, in the process, showing fairness and not favoritism.

When you do provide guidance, are you consistent or inconsistent, or does it lack follow-through? If so, you are a manager as stress producers. If you do not know where you are, then you go back to that ancient Chinese proverb that says: he who knows not and knows not that he knows not is a fool; shun him. In due time, your team members will shun you.

In my early days, yes, I was a stress producer. My last team got to know me, and I got to know them, I became a stress reducer as I learned early that it is a lot easier and better to start off as firm but fair supervisor and then get "softer "or easy. Respectful and courteous, in my conversations with them were important. I remember sharing my vison of the unit and what I wanted and what I expected of them. People, by nature, will mistake your kindness for a weakness. Why? Sometimes, it is good to show how demanding you can be so they will know that you can go there if you must. A word to the wise is sufficient.

Always be fair and just. By all means, keep a sense of humor (as appropriate, of course). I learned and experienced the forming, storming, norming and performing of a team that I had learned about in my studies. Each time a team member leaves or enters your team, you will go through these phases. You may not be in the phase for long, but you or the team will go through it. If you just became the new supervisor manager over the team, there is a good chance that someone on the team had applied for the position, which is why the most qualified for the position, sometimes, is not the best fit for the position. The hiring manager ideally would love to have both attributes in the same person. If not, the hiring manager will probably go with the best fit, more so than the most qualified.

Biloxi Management Pearl: The conventional definition of management is getting work done through people, but real management is developing people through work.

Scripture: *"Since an overseer manages God's household, he must be blameless—not overbearing, not quick-tempered, not given to drunkenness, not violent, not pursuing dishonest gain. 8 Rather, he must be hospitable, one who loves what is good, who is self-controlled, upright, holy and disciplined. 9 He must hold firmly to the trustworthy message as it has been taught so that he can encourage others by sound doctrine and refute those who oppose it."* ***(Titus 1:7-9)***

Application of Biloxi Management Pearl to the Lesson:

Personal Observation:

Developing people through work is to know the people you work with. Knowing their strengths and weaknesses and exploiting or using those strengths and building up those weaknesses.

I have had many supervisors/managers over my lifetime. Those who did this to me were not only good at what they did; they did it in a manner that I did not know it was being done.

It has probably happened to you many times, and you did not realize it. You were given an assignment or task, normally with someone else, maybe a senior member. As time went along, they started stepping back, and you started moving forward, then suddenly, the person is gone, and you are now doing all the work by yourself, both effectively and efficiently. What you were afraid of is now second nature.

Other times, the phrase that is used is baptism by fire; maybe you were the most suitable person or only person or maybe your supervisor saw something in you that let him or her know that you would figure it out. Either way, you were being developed through work, thereby making you a better person and ready for the next challenge.

How managers create stress for themselves. When managing people through work, there are a few points you must be cautious of, especially while dealing with others. Treat them with respect. Make certain that they are properly trained to do the work that has been assigned to them. Be approachable. Don't expect too much, too soon: everyone doesn't work at the same speed, so don't expect them to work at your speed. Yes, check to see how they are managing their time because poor time management is critical to getting the tasks done in a timely manner. Also, be caution of doing other people's work. They must be given the opportunity to learn, and you must have patience until they do, to a certain degree, anyway.

If you pray, don't worry, and if you worry, don't pray, is something I have always heard. However, if you worry, do so more about how it's done than the result. If it is done correctly, the results will take care of itself. Remember to delegate, at the appropriate time and to the appropriate people, giving good directions/instructions. as needed. When you do delegate, set realistic deadlines/goals/expectations, and make sure you are approachable. Learn to smile and have a good sense of humor; remember, all business is no fun. Don't take on too much, and don't become an information hoarder.

Remember to take time out for yourself and reduce their stress and yours by being an effective time manager. This includes, but is not limited to, planning ahead and delegating tasks to the appropriate person at the appropriate time. If need be, remember to take personal time off for yourself to refresh.

Seek to be fair/reasonable, focus on process (macro vs. micro) and leave work at the office. Taking work home will serve no good purpose for you or your family and will only make you a workaholic.

To truly manage people, you must master the art of empowering others/subordinates and encouraging the personal growth of employees by having realistic/achievable/smart goals. Don't forget to compliment/reward employees the best you can. One thing I remember as a supervisor/manager, I knew that I could not give raises or give them time off; however, what I could do was celebrate their birthday by taking them out to lunch. Instead of the 30-minute lunch break, we had a lunch meeting and were able to take our time and not rush. They appeared to enjoy it, and so did I. It was a time for them to let their hair down and talk to the supervisor about anything, or not.

Biloxi Management Pearl:

N – nature of the meeting (decision, info, etc.)

A – agenda

T – (when & how long)

O – outcome (desired)

Scripture: *"In everything, set them an example by doing what is good. In your teaching, show integrity, seriousness and soundness of speech that cannot be condemned so that those who oppose you may be ashamed because they have nothing bad to say about us." **(Titus 2:7-8)***

Application of Biloxi Management Pearl to the Lesson:

Personal Observation:

I learned this tidbit early in my management career. You have heard it many times, such as keep it short, sweet and to the point, keep it simple, stupid, and the like. One thing that I learned that stays with me to this day, I believe, was in a book entitled, We've Got to Start Meeting Like This: A Guide to Successful Meeting Management by Mosvick & Nelson.

After reading this book in its entirety, I changed the way I held meetings by following NATO above and one thing I never thought of was the role of the chairperson over the meeting. I remember reading that meeting topics changed every so often until you were off on a tangent. That is why meetings and conversations last so long. The chairperson's role, unless it is to impart information, is to facilitate and keep the meeting on track.

Have you ever gone into a meeting and come out with more questions than you did before the meeting? Once I learned to facilitate and not do it all, we came away with fresher ideas, and solutions.

There is a myriad of reasons why we have meetings; I would venture to say that a few of them include the following, especially if they are company or organizational meetings.

1. Sharing important company information.

2. Making key decisions or

3. requesting feedback regarding a new policy that was implemented.

4. Status meeting for providing updates on a project's status.

5. Brainstorming new ideas or solving organizational challenges.

Being the meeting facilitator is a very important position, as the facilitator must always maintain control and should not have meetings just to meet. This is not to say that you should not have a standing meeting. However, if you have a standing meeting; keep it short and sweet if there are no new developments.

Depending on the type of meeting being conducted, remember to be punctual and hand out the agenda beforehand. Since there are so many things to cover, I am going to just list these. When conducting meetings, it is best to First, check your facilitation skills and who needs to be invited to the meeting. Remember, poor facilitator skills and inviting the wrong is a recipe for disaster. Inviting the wrong people and poor facilitator skills will accomplish nothing and will end up being an unproductive meeting.

Be prepared; being unorganized/not prepared will only serve to get your meeting off to the wrong start. The facilitator should not have a hidden agenda but instead, have a clear purpose. The participants may have a hidden agenda; you probably cannot stop it, but you can minimize it. Make certain that you have an agenda and if feedback is required, that time for discussion/brainstorming is included. When and if using audio/visual, it should be used judiciously. It does not work for all occasions.

One way to do this is to be knowledgeable. If you are not knowledgeable, you will appear to be rambling, and the meeting will end up being too long. Know what is to be discussed, otherwise, you will be like the blind leading the blind. Also, if you cannot answer a question, don't be afraid to say, I don't know; I will get back to you on it. Then do it.

Establish rules of order early on, and follow them and make certain that you remind the participants to do so also. If there are no rules of order, your meeting will go south/badly very quickly.

You will have people talking over people, No resolutions/no answers at the end/conclusion of the meeting.

Once you have these tasks in order, remember to have adequate space for the number of people invited to the meeting and the information you have is the most recent. The last thing you want to do is provide misinformation, but instead the right information. This is easy to do if you have an agenda and stick to your agenda.

Stick to your agenda and have a time limit for your meeting. A long meeting, 3 hrs. or longer and you will start to lose a lot of people. If you know that the meeting is going to be longer than 90 minutes, take a quick break. Always keep in mind that being too wordy, allowing the meeting to lose focus or using big words are not wise, as well. As the facilitator, you should not get on a soapbox, and you should not let the participants do so, either. Don't "preach to the choir".

You, as the facilitator, must keep the meeting moving, stop and explore what needs to be said and then interject before it consumes or takes over or distracts from the overall purpose of the meeting. The facilitator should not be confrontational and should make certain that participants aren't either. They should make certain that they do not speak in a monotone voice and make certain to keep distractions – phones, snack bags, and jewelry, to a minimum.

The meeting facilitator must be on guard during the meeting, veering off the subject or the other participants engaging in too many sidebar conversations. Long-winded people who contribute nothing is another one. In your mind, you should have a time clock and halfway through your allotted time, if they have not started to wrap it up, kindly ask them to wrap it up. If you know of a particular person, in the meeting, who may be considered overbearing by some; make plans as to the best way to handle it. Being confrontational or causing embarrassment during a meeting is unproductive and may lead to a breakdown in productivity in future meetings, at best.

One way to avoid being confrontational or causing embarrassment is by not placing someone in the "Hot Seat". Another is something already mentioned, is by having an agenda and submitting it a day or more ahead. If the participant or participants are to speak out, they need to know well ahead of time. Also, don't worry about someone else stealing your thunder; there will be other times. Just smile and accept the praise; it may have been meant as a compliment.

Biloxi Management Pearl: Don't make your issues my (ERO) priority.

Scripture: *"For if someone does not know how to manage his own household, how will he care for God's church?" **(1 Timothy 3:5)***

Application of Biloxi Management Pearl to the Lesson:

Personal Observation:

I have used my own version of this for years, back when I was a young supervisor/manager, in my early years. As I grew older and more experienced and comfortable, I would say, when they (team members) came to me with a problem, one that I learned is that if you have a problem to go to your supervisor, for assistance. Yes, very good, I say. The other is to go a bit further, if you have a problem to go to your supervisor with the problem and an idea as how to solve the problem.

When you go to your supervisor with a problem and a solution, you are saying, I have thought about this, and this is how I would like to handle it or solve the problem. This will show the supervisor that you are a forward thinker, and it may be used. If not, it may be tweaked a little bit based on your supervisor's knowledge of similar problems encounters, or it may help her/him solve another problem that she has been thinking about; basically, you just helped your supervisor with another problem without knowing it.

Now, the other thing is that people do not mind passing off their problems to someone else if they will accept it. I have told those who I supervised that I will not make their problem my problem. I will then urge them to think about it carefully and that they should not make their applicants' problems their problems. Mainly, some people are trying to "find-an-out".

Once you take ownership of someone else's problems by rushing to assist them, it inherently becomes yours and it will erode or take away time you had planned for something else. Over time you start treating it as though it is your problem. Now, you must stop what you are doing because they have placed themselves in this predicament. There is nothing wrong with it except for (a). If you do something wrong, everybody will blame you for it, even if it is not your responsibility. And (b) if you do it and get it right, you will never get the credit you deserve for solving the problem. In the end, you will be in no man's land.

Also, don't forget if you do take on these problems, it will have babies in that more will come along, and they will grow a like cancer. Once that happens, you will become tired, apathetic, and not a fun person to be around. It (other people's problems) will start to take its toll on you, your health, and your family, and ultimately, it will take on a life of its own. You will have that albatross around your neck.

Best solution: Listen to the problem and what is being said. If it is their problem, let them figure it out. If not, and you provide an answer, they will blame you if it does not work. All people are not your friends. Just saying.

I only step in and be a supervisor/manager and make it my issue when need be. Normally, when the character, integrity, etc., of the organization or myself is at stake.

So, in the words of doing drugs and alcohol, and other vices, learn to "stop before you start". If it has no bearing on you or it will not change anything about you or your life over the short or long term, leave it alone. It is their problem; let them solve it. If you want to help, coach, delegate, assist, counsel, or do whatever you can, don't be rushed to do something just because they did not do their due diligence and don't make their problem your problems, and don't make their issues your priority.

I am a strong believer in, if you don't include me in the beginning, (or what got you in this jam), don't include me in the end. I remember I was working at one position when we (our supervisor and one of my peers) were called into a meeting. The executive director asked us about our thoughts about one of his deputy directors, with whom he was having problems. After he said what he had to say, I questioned him as to why he hired the two directors and if he had done his due diligence beforehand. His reply was that he had only hired one, and the other he inherited from the last administration. That one I gave him a pass on, as I knew that these are "will and pleasure" positions and that he did not have to keep the deputy director from the last administration. He could have requested his resignation, terminated him or requested that he/she reapply for the position. In essence, by default, he hired him.

After a few more questions and answers and as we were about to leave, I did what I normally do when I think it was a crazy meeting, I started to laugh to myself. My supervisor and my peer looked at me. The executive director then asked what I was laughing at, and that he was serious and that I was laughing at him (he was a former military officer, so he was probably not used to this). So, I looked at him, and since he called me out, I politely stated that I didn't understand. You hired him; of all the people in the agency, you hired him? You did not bother to look at his people skills, work habits, and other skills prior to appointing him to this position, and now you are asking us our thoughts. I could have told you beforehand, you would not be having these problems. I saw this a long time ago; I was on the interview team when he interviewed for a lower-class position.

There are people who interview well, but you can tell there was something not right. The interview team selected someone else. He was eventually hired by another department in the agency. In less than 3 years, he was promoted from a specialist to a director, and then you created a position just for him. Now you are asking us, what is wrong? The meeting was adjourned, and we left.

I must admit, I was thinking if I was going to be written up, but two things I had going for me, at the time. 1. He asked the question I just answered, and 2. I was planning on retiring anyway. Ultimately, I saw that this was his problem; they kept giving in to the "deputy director's" every whim from the time he was hired there. In 3 years promoted from a specialist to deputy director, only in America. As one of my former coworkers said, "his meteoric rise to success".

Biloxi Management Pearl: "Our prime purpose in this life is to help others. And if you can't help them, at least don't hurt them." H.H. Dalai Lama

Scripture: *"The end of the matter; all has been heard. Fear God and keep his commandments, for this is the whole duty of man."*
(Ecclesiastes 12:13)

Application of Biloxi Management Pearl to the Lesson:

Personal Observation:

Do managers/supervisors have the power to help or hurt? This is a very good saying, and in management /supervision, you can help or hurt them by using a management style that is not right for that person/team member.

Now, according to the literature, there are four management styles. There may be more, but let's go with these four: telling and directing, delegating, participating and supporting, and coaching and selling. The belief is that you must know your team member, and by knowing your team member, is to help him/her to grow and be productive. Using the wrong style on the wrong person will hurt them.

Each of these styles may be used on the same person at different times or the same person all the time. Again, the goal is to analyze each separate situation, and determine which business management style fits best for that person at that time.

Remember that choosing the appropriate management style requires balancing tasks and relationships. Using a telling and directing style on a person who only needs coaching and selling may hurt the person's self-esteem. Equally so, whereas using delegating to a person who has the initiative helps the person to grow.

I remember in my early days as a junior supervisor, I was and still am an introvert. Keep in mind that I have brothers who are very extroverted, and I learned that if you want to run with the big dogs, you must learn to hold your own. Say what you mean and mean what you say, and move on. No time for self-reflecting and thinking hard, so as I like to tell people, I am a learned extrovert, so much so that when I took the Myers-Briggs Type Indicator way back then, I was told that they had never seen anyone who was dead even in all categories. I made a joke about it and said that during that time, the management side of George was slowly taking on the personal side of George.

During my first week on the new job in the field of mental health, I had a resident who was acting out. When the staff told my superior what was going on, she looked at me and said, that is George's resident/client. George, take care of it, and I did.

During that same period, I was having my first Treatment Team meeting, and the Resident Supervisor, an older woman, started drilling me. And then she asked, do you know your residents/clients, and she stated, you need to learn all your residents/clients. After the meeting, she called me to the side and said, George, whenever you go into a meeting, be prepared for anything that may come at you.

Those ladies did what they did to make me a better manager/supervisor. They helped me by doing what they did, and then they explained why they did it; basically, true leaders must first analyze the needs of their subordinates.

Now, I am going to fast forward to my last supervisor as an experienced supervisor. I remember once, I had a subordinate employee. She was working on her bachelor's degree, I knew she had, so there was no problem there. The problem she came to me with was this one particular course she was taking was offered only during the daytime (working hours) and would require her to be away from the office a couple of hours a week. Yes, she could have used her leave time, which would soon run out and then would use leave without pay, and that would create problems with human resources.

The solution, she would submit her weekly schedule as to when she would be away from the office and for how long. Most importantly, when would she make those hours up, coming in early, staying late, what have you. My main concern was that she put in her 8 hours per workday and that her work did not suffer, as a result. It all worked out. Her work never suffered as a result. We had a great team that did not mind helping each other.

Did her other teammates help her when there was a deadline, I really don't know, nor did I care. The reason being, as I have said before, they always came through, when I asked them for anything.

Why did I do it, and why was it so easy to decide to assist her? Well, one should never hinder one from trying to better themselves, if possible. The other reason, God prepared me for that moment. You see, when I was working on my master's degree, the same thing or similar happened to me. My supervisor (TK, as I called her) did the exact same thing for me. (Thank you, Jesus, Thank You Lord and Thank you for giving me a supervisor like TK)

Now, to me it was about giving back, and it was not to do hurt or harm but to help. My actions were that if you want or need my assistance, we can discuss it. Sometimes, we must meet people where they are.

I remember another incident where another one of my team members went off and told me what she would not do. My reply was "okay". She came back the next day, and she apologized, and she had already done what I had asked. She later asked me how I knew she was going to do it. Why didn't you write me up? My reply was, I didn't know, and I would have. I could have done it the assigned task myself or I could have reassigned it to someone else. I probably would have myself, if it was not completed by the time, I thought you should have completed it or when I started to do it myself, I would have written you up. Just that simple.

We have both left that place of employment, but we still stay in contact with each other. We just had a former team member to pass away. When I heard of her passing, among many things that we talked about, one came back crystal clear. She asked me one day, as only she can, George, how do you deal/put up with all of these strong-willed women? I looked at her and the rest of the women standing around me, and I replied, I don't let you bother me." Rest in Peace, ADS.

Biloxi Management Pearl: It's not what happens to you that determines how far you will go in life; it is how you handle what happens to you.

Scripture: "And without faith, it is impossible to please him, for whoever would draw near to God must believe that he exists and that he rewards those who seek him." (Hebrews 11:6)

Application of Biloxi Management Pearl to the Lesson:

Personal Observation:

Now, this is reminiscent of "I am the master of my fate; I am the captain of my soul." You may have heard of it; these are the last (I think) two lines from William Ernest Henley's poem 'Invictus '. Now, for those of us who have read it, it discusses or provides advice to those who blame God for their failures. It is not only about God but the attitude that makes the person want to give up when faced with challenges. We all have and go through the trials and tribulations of life.

Challenges make one stronger, but mentally submitting oneself to those impediments extinguishes the inner light that one carries inside the heart from infancy. Through these lines, Henley tried to say that it's not about how difficult the path is; it's about one's attitude to keep moving forward without submitting oneself to fate's recourse.

During your lifetime, you will be thrown many curved balls, there will be many dropped passes, and occasionally, you may hit a buzzer-beater or a hole-in-one, regardless of whether it is the thrill of victory or the agony of defeat. We all go through some things. It is after we have gone through those things that we must pick up those stumbling blocks and make them our stepping stones.

Our stepping stones to God and what he has for you and your life. As the saying goes, when life serves you lemons, make lemonade. If the lemonade is too bitter, you can make it sweeter. In other words, you determine how you will handle what happens to you.

When handling those bad things in life, I remember this statement written on a billboard that said those bad things in life are meant to make you better, not bitter, whether it is on the job, at home, or where you are. That boss is riding you; that manager did not give you the promotion you thought you deserved. Your girlfriend/boyfriend left you for someone new? You did not get the grade or into the college/university you wanted to get in to?

It appears that everything you touch seems to be going south, friends are leaving you, money is getting low, and there appears to be no relief in sight. For all those things, continue to trust God if you don't already, start to trust God. Will it make your life better? The question is, by trusting in him, will it make your life worse? However, what I can say about it is this: even if trusting and believing in him and trusting in, his word does not make your life better or the situation that you find yourself in better, it will make you feel better about your life or will make you feel better about the situation that you find yourself in

Life has meaning; your life has meaning, and you are here for a purpose, whether you believe it or not. It will be revealed to you in due time. In the meantime, remember that he (God) has you. Think and be positive.

When you think positive, things will start to look positive, and you will start getting those positive vibes. That is when life throws you a curveball, or you drop a pass. But if you remember that by thinking positive thoughts, you will realize that this is not the first pass of the first game of the first play of the game; it cannot and will not define who you are, who you are and what you will become.

As I stated earlier, if you are going through some things, remember to pick up those stumbling blocks and make them your stepping stones. Remember, it's not what happens to you that determines how far you will go in life; it is how you handle what happens to you.

Last point: God has you.

"Be strong and courageous. Do not be afraid or terrified because of them, for the Lord your God goes with you; he will never leave you nor forsake you." **(Deuteronomy 31:6)**

Hosea 4:6 (KJV)

"My people are destroyed for lack of knowledge: because thou hast rejected knowledge, I will also reject thee, that thou shalt be no priest to me: seeing thou hast forgotten the law of thy God, I will also forget thy children."

By highlighting the crucial value of information, especially knowledge of God, this passage underlines the significance of knowledge for both survival and benefits. A lack of information may lead to disaster, which underlines the power and significance of being well-informed. It also highlights the fact that ignorance can lead to catastrophe. It is often believed that having information, particularly spiritual understanding, is an essential component of living a successful and satisfying life. Understanding and insight are not only advantageous; rather, they are necessary for avoiding traps and gaining benefits, as this passage implies. When people are lacking in information, especially awareness of the principles and direction that God provides, they are more likely to make judgments that result in unfavorable results. It is important to note that ignorance in this context is not just a lack of knowledge; rather, it is a perilous blank that may lead to behaviors that are erroneous and, ultimately, disastrous.

Understanding God's character, His commands, and His promises are all components of what it means to have knowledge of God for Christians. This in-depth, personal understanding serves as a basis for making smart choices, growing resilience in the face of adversities, and creating a life that is in alignment with the purposes of the divine. It suggests that gaining an understanding of the will of God and putting His precepts into practice in one's everyday life may result in both spiritual and financial success. In a more general sense, the poem may also be interpreted to mean that it is essential to have a comprehensive understanding of all aspects of one's life. Individuals who possess knowledge are better able to make decisions that are based on accurate information, efficiently solve issues, and negotiate the intricacies of life with more agility. Being informed is beneficial in both professional and personal situations since it enables one to anticipate and mitigate risks, seize opportunities, and accomplish objectives.

A further point to consider is that this poem emphasizes the repercussions of ignorance. People are more prone to make the same errors; they are also more likely to be misled by false information, and they are less likely to reap the advantages that come with having insight and wisdom when they do not seek out or respect knowledge. This has the potential to result in a cycle of unfavorable results, which will not only have an impact on people but also on their communities and on society as a whole. For those in positions of authority, this passage serves as a potent reminder of the significance of lifelong education and the never-ending quest for knowledge. Those in leadership positions who make the acquisition and dissemination of information a priority are able to more effectively direct their teams, encourage creativity, and create settings in which informed decision-making is the norm. This dedication to knowledge has the potential to result in businesses that are more resilient, flexible, and financially successful.

Biloxi Management Pearl: Good management is the art of making problems so interesting and their solutions so constructive that everyone wants to get to work and deal with them.

Scripture: "Let us not become weary in doing good, for at the proper time we will reap a harvest if we do not give up."
(Galatians 6:9)

Application of Biloxi Management Pearl to the Lesson:

Personal Observation:

We all have rules or sayings that keep us grounded. A very good management strategy. As a supervisor/manager, you must get buy-in from everyone in order for it to work. Remember, you should treat everyone as equals, share the credit, and, in the end, don't worry about who gets the credit. My last team, before I retired, made this one come true for me (Ashea, Melissa, Darla, Ashley, and Patricia, you know who you are). I had several sayings, two sayings in particular. I have more, but these two are the most profound to me anyways. The first saying is, "I believe that work should be fun, and I am going to do my best to make and keep it that way." The second one was to remember that it is a thankless position; when you are doing your job and helping our stakeholders, and everything is going well, they (stakeholders) will love you to death, and as soon as something comes up and you tell them that because of policy, regulations, etc. that they cannot do it they will turn on you. This is the nature of the beast in which we serve." Now, being the practical joker that I am, they first had to buy into and trust the process. Once they did, we did, and for 6-7 years, we were arguably the best team in the agency. Interesting, to the point that I believe it is because I allowed them to be them.

Management and supervisors' ultimate job is to get the job done; the second is to prepare to bridge that gap/or divide from where you are to where you are going or want to be. The use of delegation coaching prepares the individuals as such. If they can develop the skill set, you want to coach it; on the other hand, if they already have the skill set, you want to nurture and delegate toward it. You want it to be so mild that it is happening to them, and they don't even realize it.

You ask for their opinion and buy into the process, listening and paying attention to their thought process. As managers, you don't want to have to pull rank unless you must. This is best done by admitting that you don't have all the answers. When those who work with you on your team (for the most part) realize that you are being genuine and you indeed want their input and value their decision and decision-making skills in seeking solutions, it appeals to others to want to work and assist. This is the starting point of synergy.

Synergy is established. They understand that you are the supervisor manager and that you will have the last say so, or upper management does anyway. But you know how to word what they have given you to give to upper management. Synergy

Yes, synergy is developed and with that, there are more solutions so constructive that everyone wants to get to work and deal with them. They are being heard, valued, and understood then that you, as the manager, can take a step back and allow those in the know to do what they do best: lead. In the process, you do what you do best, allow them to come into their own, and lead when the time comes for their own special project. You have, in essence, allowed them to shine. You are no longer the shadow over them; you have now become the wind beneath their wings.

Biloxi Management Pearl: "Even a blind squirrel finds a nut." Sid Melton

*Scripture: "But my God shall supply all your need according to his riches in glory by Christ Jesus." **(Philippians 4:19)***

Application of Biloxi Management Pearl to the Lesson:

Personal Observation:

So, do good things happen to us because we are lucky or blessed? Does the blind squirrel find the nut because of luck or blessing? Merriam defines luck as a force that brings good fortune or <u>adversity</u>, or the events or circumstances that operate for or against an individual, then maybe a favoring chance. Blessing, if you believe in God and the bible, tends to be more associated with protection, happiness and the like. If we really truly think about it, God's blessings are meant to assist us in navigating this thing we call life: the bible and the Holy Spirit, which Jesus left as a Comforter upon his ascension to Heaven, guide us to a path of righteousness.

So, if you supervise by luck or chance, you will surely get it right sometimes. In that instance, you are doing the right thing. As a manager, you have no idea what you are doing or what you are supposed to be doing. If you keep at it, you will soon figure it out and get it correct or surround yourself with someone who will. Those people who believe and trust in God and his word

Our Sunday School Teacher/facilitator is not good; in my opinion, he is great. He has shared things with us and, in the process, taught me a lot of things, as well as the rest of my Sunday School Classmates. Our Sunday school teachers/facilitator stated that he does not believe in luck, but instead, in blessings.

Even a blind squirrel finds a nut. So, this is alluding to the fact that the squirrel will be lucky enough to find the nut by happenstance. So, it is not by luck that the blind squirrel finds a nut to feed himself; it is a blessing. Think about it: **(Matthew 6:26)** says Behold the fowls of the air: for they sow not, neither do they reap, nor gather into barns; yet your heavenly Father feedeth them. Are ye not much better than they? Yes, I agree there is no such thing as luck; they are blessings. Imagine, if you will, if the whole world or, at a minimum, all of God's children (we are all his creation, whether you believe it or not, but we are not all his children) would believe in blessings and not luck. It is not luck that you got that promotion or that new car, job, or house. It is not luck that you barely missed that accident; it is not luck that you and your family made it to where you are now. It is not luck that you graduated or found the person of your dreams. No, be bold and call it what it is; they are blessings from God. Be happy and in good spirits!!

I listened and now remember what our Sunday school facilitator told us about what his parents taught him (his Pearls), and he, in turn, has passed them on to us. Even at this age, I am still learning. I will end this with a few more words: I have been and will continue to be blessed to learn from all my Sunday School Classmates. Their pearls continue to smooth out my rough edges. I truly understand the movie It's a Wonderful Life; what I hear from my classmates are pearls of wisdom that they have heard and passed on to them, and now they are passing it on to us, and we are passing it on to our family and friends.

Thank God for your many blessings; I have, and I will continue to do so. Our Sunday School Facilitator Derek Polk, transitioned before this book was published. I learned a lot from him, and he is missed. But as you can tell, his words live on. Rest in Peace DP!

Theological Perspectives:

Biblical Examples:

1. Joseph's Rise to Power in Egypt:

A significant illustration of the action of divine providence may be found in the tale of Joseph. Joseph's brothers, who were envious of him, sold him into slavery, which may have been considered an extremely unfortunate circumstance. However, he was able to ascend to a position of tremendous influence in Egypt by means of a sequence of occurrences that may be interpreted as nothing more than a series of coincidences. One may argue that his ability to decipher the dreams of the Pharaoh, which ultimately led to his appointment as second-in-command, was a stroke of good fortune or blessings. On the other hand, Joseph himself recognized the guidance of God throughout his trip. In the book of Genesis, chapter 50, verse 20, Joseph is recorded as stating to his brothers, "You intended to harm me, but God intended it for good to accomplish what is now being done, the saving of many lives." This story emphasizes that what may seem to be random luck is often a sign of God's meticulous purpose, even if it may appear to be random.

2. David's Victory over Goliath:

David's defeat of Goliath is another event that might be attributed to a blessing. A young shepherd boy defeating a giant warrior with a single stone seems improbable. Yet, David attributed his victory not to chance but to God's intervention. In 1 Samuel 17:45-47, David declares, "You come against me with sword and spear and javelin, but I come against you in the name of the Lord Almighty… This day, the Lord will deliver you into my hands." David's faith and reliance on God exemplify how divine providence operates, turning what might seem like a lucky break into a clear act of divine blessing.

3. Esther's Favor with the King:

Esther's rise to become queen and her role in saving the Jewish people from genocide might also be seen as a fortunate series of events. Yet, the Book of Esther emphasizes the underlying divine orchestration. Mordecai's advice to Esther in **(Esther 4:14)**, "And who knows but that you have come to your royal position for such a time as this?" highlights the belief in a purposeful divine plan rather than mere luck.

4. Paul's Conversion on the Road to Damascus:

Paul's dramatic conversion from a persecutor of Christians to a devoted apostle might be considered a fortunate turning point. However, **(Acts 9:3-6)** details a clear divine intervention, with a vision of Christ leading to his transformation. This event underscores the notion that life-changing moments are often divinely orchestrated rather than random occurrences.

Theology of Providence:

1. Concept of Divine Providence:

Divine providence refers to God's governance and care over creation. Christian theology asserts that God is actively involved in the world, guiding and sustaining all things towards His divine purpose. This belief suggests that what appears to be luck is actually part of God's meticulous plan.

2. Framework of Understanding Luck and Blessings:

God's Sovereignty: Divine providence is rooted in the belief that God is sovereign and has ultimate control over the universe. This means that nothing happens by chance; rather, every event is part of God's intentional design. **(Proverbs 16:9)** states, "In their hearts, humans plan their course, but the Lord establishes their steps."

Purposeful Events: According to this view, events that seem fortunate or coincidental are seen as God's way of providing for and guiding His people. **(Romans 8:28)** reinforces this, stating, "And we know that in all things God works for the good of those who love him, who have been called according to his purpose."

Human Perception: While humans might perceive certain events as luck due to their unpredictable nature, faith in divine providence encourages believers to trust that there is a divine reason behind every occurrence, even if it is not immediately apparent.

3. Implications for Believers:

Trust and Faith: Belief in divine providence encourages trust in God's plan, especially during uncertain times. It provides comfort that God is in control and working towards a greater good.

Gratitude: Recognizing events as blessings rather than luck fosters a sense of gratitude towards God. Believers are encouraged to see their lives as filled with divine purpose and intentionality.

Active Participation: While acknowledging God's control, believers are also called to actively participate in God's plan through prayer, obedience, and good works. This cooperative dynamic underscore the balance between divine sovereignty and human responsibility.

Biloxi Management Pearl: Obstacles are those frightful things you see when you take your eyes off your goals.

Scripture: "They will fight against you, but they will not overcome you, for I am with you to deliver you," declares the Lord. (Jeremiah 1:19)

Application of Biloxi Management Pearl to the Lesson:

Personal Observation:

This is reminiscent of what our professor used to tell us during our matriculation for the doctorate. "Keep your eyes on the prize."

Yes, and those frightful things are all around us. Those obstacles may be in the form of family, school, work, friends, money, debt, children or yes, even us/ourselves. Sometimes, we don't know how to get out of our own way.

Make a decision and stay focused. Once you make a decision to do something or make/set a goal, you must make it your 2nd priority. Second Priority? Then what is 1st priority? What is more important to you and why? If it is important, why is it second? These are very good questions; God should be your 1st priority. If you do what is pleasing to him, everything or all other goals, objectives, etc., will work out just fine. Remember, I can do all things through Christ Jesus, who strengthens me. Also, don't forget to have faith that if he (God) brings you to it, he will bring you through it.

As I am writing this segment, we are studying Faith in Hebrews in our Sunday School Lesson. So, again you must have faith that those frightful little things that are there, you should turn a blind eye to them. If you do happen to see them, then ask God to help you get around or go through them (Don't move my mountain but give me the strength to climb.)

Why not just ask God to move them? Well, as frightful as they can be/maybe, sometimes, they are there for a reason. Keep in mind that these obstacles or stumbling blocks can be useful. If we take a moment and look at these obstacles or stumbling blocks that tend to be in our way, we listen to the voice of God. God can and will direct our path if we listen and faint not. He can direct our paths as to how we can position those stumbling blocks and make them our stepping stones.

When I was young, I remember listening to a song that said, my stumbling blocks are now my stepping stones. So, just thinking about it in this light, we have gone from no way out to a way out just by listening to the voice of God. Making God our number 1 priority and our primary Goal the 2nd priority. Now, we can say don't move my mountain, but give me the strength to climb with conviction. Now, those frightful little things are no longer frightful; we are now able to use them to our advantage.

Where did it all start? It started with Faith. Faith in God, Faith that we can do it and faith that he will do it if it is what God wants for you.

My goal was to become an officer in the United States Army. A PhD was nowhere in my mind. I remember talking to my grandmother Martha years ago, and she stated the army isn't for everyone and my reply was, neither is college. I now know that she knew something that I did not know.

In management or as supervisors, we must remain focused on what is ahead of us as well as what is going on around us. We, as supervisors/managers, cannot allow ourselves to become too distracted by those frightful things called obstacles or our stumbling blocks, as we are continuously being pulled in various directions. Those who look for us for guidance and need our assistance and those to whom we report who want and expect more of us to better the organization.

So, as the saying goes, the devil is in the details, so the devil is in those frightful little things that we call obstacles that tend to take us away from our real duty or our real number one priority. When it happens to you, just pray to God for strength, have faith, and he will change those obstacles and stumbling blocks into your stepping stones.

Those obstacles may be in the form of co-workers, who mean you know good, subordinates or supervisors in the workplace. Just remember to relax, remain focused, keep God first and enjoy life.

Why, you ask, because the bible says that we will succeed if we faint not. "And let us not be weary in well doing: for in due season we shall reap if we faint not." **(Galatians 6:9 KJV).**

Just Saying.

Biloxi Management Pearl: "Correction does much, but encouragement does more.

Encouragement after censure is as the sun after a shower." Goethe

Scripture: "Wherefore comfort yourselves together, and edify one another, even as also ye do." (1 Thessalonians 5:11)

Application of Biloxi Management Pearl to the Lesson:

Personal Observation:

Correction comes from the root word Correct. It is a passive-active word that you are doing something after the fact. Merriam defines correction as the action or an instance of correcting such as, among other things, rebuke or punishment: a bringing into conformity with a standard. Here, the deed has been done, and now the supervisor/manager is pointing out the error of the person's ways. To admonish the person for doing something that he or she may not have known what was being done.

Would it not be better if we had words of encouragement?

Encouragement comes from the root word encourage...it is an active word; Merriam defines it as the act of making something more appealing or more likely to happen or something that makes someone more determined, hopeful, or confident. Praise or praiseworthy are other words I tend to think of. I see encouragement as a person standing side by side, guiding them, assisting them, and helping along the way. Helping them to "keep their eyes on the prize," don't be sidetracked by those little annoyances around you; they can do you no good. Focus on the voice and the words that are being said.

I remember hearing or reading, "What shall we then say to these things? If God be for us, who can be against us?" **(Romans 8:31-KJV).** God is for us, then who can be against us? We must become more Christ-like; we should seek to understand and then to be understood. We should seek to encourage our fellow men and women first and correct less. Encouragement is leading, helping and building up one another. We, as supervisors, should seek to encourage our fellow men and women to do their utmost best to become all that God wants them to be. Correcting and showing someone the error of their ways is good; however, in my opinion, encouragement is better.

As a Christian, there is nothing better than encouragement. Acknowledging that you believe in them and that God has them, he is always there, and he is waiting on you.

I remember that we had a young lady in church, and she stated that she wanted to be baptized. She stated that she believed in God, but she had slid back into her old life, or she was back in the world. The pastor asked her if she had repented and asked for forgiveness, and she stated that she had, but she was coming up and asking for help. The pastor told her if you had repented and asked for forgiveness, he (God) had already forgiven you; he was waiting on you.

The pastor was encouraging her to move forward, once you asked for forgiveness, it is time to move on and do better and be better. It is so easy to correct a person, but what the person really needs is encouragement.

The Bible states, "For God hath not given us the spirit of fear; but of power, and of love, and of a sound mind." **(2 Timothy 1:7)**. Now, use that power and love to encourage and build others up. You will reap many rewards.

When encouraging and building others up, sometimes, all you will need is the word to change that person's life around for the better. I remember sitting on the steps at a military installation in my early 20s, waiting for my fate. I was in a dark place that became darker day by day. For the first time, as an adult I was facing failure that I had no control over. Everything that I was doing or had done had gone wrong. The harder I tried, the worse it got. Here I was with my head in my hand, sitting on those steps. An officer in his green dress greens walked up and stood in front of me. No making me salute him, etc. He stood there for a few seconds, and he said, no matter what you are going through, just remember, it will not be like this always. Then he walked away. As I pondered and thought about what I was going through and what he had said, I stood up and turned around to thank him for the words of encouragement. All I could see was his patented leather shoes as it walked through the door. I have never looked back since then. What is odd is that I don't remember what those storms and dark places were specifically, what it was about or what the outcome was. However, I do remember those words of encouragement when I needed them most.

Whoever you are, wherever you are, I thank God, and I thank God for you.

Thank you!!

Biloxi Management Pearl: A bird doesn't fly just because it has wings....it has wings, so it can fly!

Scripture: "For whatever is born of God overcomes the world; and this is the victory that has overcome the world—our faith."
(1 John 5:4)

Application of Biloxi Management Pearl to the Lesson:

Personal Observation:

When I place this quote in terms of management and supervision, I look at it in terms of skillsets. We don't supervise because we have the skillset; we have the skillset, so we can supervise. This goes back to the question of whether leaders are born or made.

Have you ever thought about why you decided to become or want to become a supervisor/manager? When I graduated from college, I thought I had the education and the talents and skills (or so I thought at that time anyway) that I should be the leader that I was born to be. I thought it was my calling, and, of course, the money was better.

Many years later, while looking back to a point when my sister and I were having a conversation about supervisors/managers, I asked her (after she had been working at this one place for 10-15 years, at least) why she did not apply for one of the supervisors/managerial position at the workplace that were open to her. (I mean, apply, even if you don't get it, right?). Her reply was that she did not want to have to tell people what to do. This led to a longer deeper conversation about supervision and management. I tried to explain that supervision is not telling people what to do. For the most part, in the workplace, most people already know what their job description is and from that, what they are supposed to do. The position of a supervisor manager, for the most part, is to make certain that those under you, your team members, are doing what they are supposed to do, when they are supposed to do it, where and how they're supposed to do it. Most importantly, that it is done correctly, and on time, depending, on the nature of the job.

Basically, the supervisor/manager is to adhere to the rules, regulations and policies as set forth by the organization. But telling people what to do, no, they already know what to do, or should anyway. It wasn't until my later years and as a more seasoned supervisor/manager that I learned our true purpose of becoming supervisor leaders/managers.

However, before moving on to that point, let's look at man's role in general if we look at **(Psalms 8:6-8 in KJV)**. Thou madest him to have dominion over the works of thy hands; thou hast put all things under his feet: 7. All sheep and oxen, yea, and the beasts of the field; 8. The fowl of the air, and the fish of the sea, and whatsoever passeth through the paths of the seas. 9 O LORD our

Lord, how excellent is thy name in all the earth! And Genesis 1:26 "And God said, let us make man in our image, after our likeness: and let them have dominion over the fish of the sea, and over the fowl of the air, and over the cattle, and over all the earth, and over every creeping thing that creepeth upon the earth." Now, if we look at this in this light, we should use these same talents, skills, etc., to make certain that those whom we are supposed to be supervising, (team members) are following and adhering to the policies and regulations. Not only ensuring that they are doing what they are supposed to be doing in accordance with the organization's policies and procedures, but it should go beyond that. Yes, because ultimately, we are our brother's keeper.

As our brother's keeper, we should use the opportunities/responsibilities given to us by God to lead others to God. No, not by preaching to them, but through compassion, understanding, empathy, and letting them know that no matter what they are going through. If they believe and have faith in God and in our Lord and Savior, Jesus Christ, all things will work for the best for those who believe.

At some point, as a supervisor /manager, you will be faced with questions and or concerns from your team members. Sometimes, as a supervisor/manager, you will need to counsel, coach, delegate, lead, instruct, and sometimes all with the same person and or day. When it arises, where will your faith take you? The question then becomes, do you have the skillset, be it innate or learned?

Biloxi Management Pearl: You speak volumes by the way you listen.

Scripture: "Wherefore, my beloved brethren, let every man be swift to hear, slow to speak, slow to wrath: for the wrath of man worketh not the righteousness of God." (James 1:19-20)

Application of Biloxi Management Pearl to the Lesson:

Personal Observation:

Speaking volumes is saying a lot about a person, place, thing, character, or observation without saying a word or few words, at best. Being a supervisor/manager is not and should not be just about talking in meetings and directing subordinate personnel. It is more about how one carries him or herself, always.

Providing a listening ear to understand what is going on in their lives, how their family is doing, and how is work on the project going, etc. Being able to understand their needs is the true meaning and creed criteria of a good supervisor/manager.

When we listen to the person, be it problems, comments, concerns, or whatever and just listen to them when they want to be heard. It may be to help them focus on something or to help them work through a problem, and yes, sometimes, just a listening ear, sounding board, if you will, to be heard. Even when they want to talk about their family and friends, they just want a good listening ear.

We as humans have a need to be heard, and we, as supervisors/managers, can fulfill that need (at the appropriate time, of course). We can show empathy; we can show that we care about them as individuals who have lives outside of the workplace. We, for the most part, want them to do better, and they, in turn, want to do better. They are not robots to be programmed, devoid of all emotions and just there to do our, the organization's bidding. This was the norm way back when.

As I think back, I remember from my studies (organization and organization theory) that back in the 1940s, workers were seen and viewed as robots devoid of emotions, etc. Times have changed since then, and so have we, as supervisors/leaders.

In my last years as a supervisor/manager, I started to understand more about active listening. I worked mostly with females, strong-willed females, at that. I also remember one of them asking me how I "work with all these strong-willed females/ladies." My reply was, "I don't let what you or they say or do get next to me." Case in point: one day, one of the ladies came into my office going off. The strange thing about this is that I truly don't remember why or what she was talking about. All I remember was calmly sitting at my desk when she came in, with her voice raised and standing. I never said a word; I just looked at her as she continued to go off. When she came up for air, I motioned toward the empty chair for her to have a seat (as in, have a seat). She stopped long enough to say, I don't want to sit down, and she continued to go off, and after about 30-45 seconds, I again motioned her to have a seat. She continued to ramble on, and then, for the 3rd time, I motioned toward the chair for her to have a seat. After the 3rd time, she had a seat. After she had a seat, I calmly and politely asked her, now, what is it you want to talk to me about? She calmed down and then started to talk. She did not have that much to say, from what I remember, and we worked everything out. She never came to me in that manner again, and yes, she did apologize, non-needed, I stated, I understand. The point is or was that I am not going to listen to her while she stand over me and talk to me, with her voice raised. Could I have written her up? Yes, but what would that have accomplished? Could I have stood up? Yes, then that would have made it look adversarial and possibly gotten out of hand over what, in my mind, was trivial. Wherefore, my beloved brethren, let every man be swift to hear, slow to speak, slow to wrath: for the wrath of man worketh not the righteousness of God **(James 1:19-20)**

I remember another incident when another one of my team members came in. She, too, was venting and talking about what she was not going to do and a few other things (no cursing or profanity, of course). Much like the other incident, I calmly looked at her. After she finished, she left. Yes, she did the work as assigned and on time. When she came back, we talked again, as usual. I remember telling her my belief. Two things here on my beliefs: one, "If you do what you are supposed to do, I will not do what I have to do." The other one, I don't believe in making your problem my problem; I have enough of my own to deal with. Now, if you want to, I will give you some of my problems".

Yes, I worked with some strong-willed females back then. We got along very well; we got to know and understand each other. I could ask them to do anything (work related) at any time and they would do it, even at the 11th hour. Don't get me wrong, they would complain, but they never let me down. They would tell me during our time together that they remember when they came to me with a problem; I could always make them feel better about it. I would use a quick joke to get their mind off it, or something to lighten up the load and lighten the mood, and my saying these words, "Just remember, don't let their problem become your problem."

At times, I reflect or conduct a self-assessment. I realized that I had come full circle. I had started to really explore active listening. I went beyond hearing what was being said or just listening to what was being said, but I had gone a bit further, to actively listening, to what was being said. Try it, you may be surprised by the results. Enough said.

Exploration of Active Listening

<u>Definition and Importance:</u> Listening actively is a dynamic communication approach that requires the listener to be fully engaged and present during the whole conversation. It is not the same as passive listening; rather, it requires people to totally immerse themselves in the discussion by fully focusing, comprehending, reacting, and recalling what is being said. In order to fully concentrate, one must give the person who is speaking complete attention, put aside any distractions, and keep a concentrated awareness of the words and non-verbal clues that they are using. The demonstration of respect and attention that this exhibit helps to create an atmosphere that is favorable to open communication and mutual comprehension. Understanding is an essential component of active listening, which involves activities other than just hearing the words being said. Therefore, it is necessary for listeners to probe deeper into the information that the speaker is conveying, recognizing subtleties in tone, mood, and body language. It is possible for active listeners to comprehend the underlying meaning that lies behind the words that are stated if they empathize with the viewpoint and purpose of the speaker.

Active listening requires the listener to provide feedback to the person who is speaking, demonstrate that they have comprehended what they are saying, and validate their views and emotions. This may be accomplished by the use of non-verbal signals, such as keeping eye contact and nodding, as well as vocal confirmations, such as paraphrasing or summarizing essential themes. Respect and interest are communicated via such responsive conduct, which in turn helps to develop trust and rapport between persons. Remembering is the last component of active listening, which involves the listener retaining significant information from the discussion for the purpose of future reference. This not only demonstrates that you are paying attention and respecting the person who is speaking, but it also makes it easier to effectively follow up and put into action any ideas or activities that have been addressed.

When it comes to the dynamics of a team, the significance of attentive listening cannot be stressed. It is a foundational component in the process of establishing trust and rapport among members of the team, so fostering an atmosphere that is conducive to collaboration and support. People are more willing to speak freely, exchange ideas, and successfully work with one another in order to achieve shared objectives when they have the sense that they are being given true attention and understanding. Additionally, active listening contributes to the development of empathy and comprehension, which in turn improves interpersonal relationships and the settlement of conflicts within teams. Team members acquire more empathy and are better able to negotiate differences and problems in a constructive manner when they actively engage with the opinions and experiences of other members of the team.

Techniques: For the purpose of enabling a more profound level of participation and comprehension during talks, active listening comprises a variety of strategies. To demonstrate attention, understanding, and engagement, these strategies include nodding, keeping eye contact, summarizing what the speaker has said, and asking open-ended questions. Each of these techniques plays a significant part in exhibiting these qualities. Through the use of a non-verbal indication known as nodding, one might convey agreement, acknowledgment, or comprehension. Listeners give the impression that they are actively participating in the discussion and support the contributions made by the speaker when they nod in response to the points that are being made by the speaker. Taking this uncomplicated action helps to build rapport with the speaker and encourages them to continue expressing their views and experiences.

Another crucial active listening method that displays sincerity, attention, and respect is simply maintaining eye contact with the person you are listening to. It is important for listeners to convey that they are paying undivided attention and that they are really interested in what is being said by establishing direct eye contact with the speaker. This visual connection helps people build a feeling of trust and connection with one another, which in turn improves the quality of conversation and fosters a deeper understanding. For the purpose of confirming comprehension and ensuring that all parties have the same understanding, summarizing what the speaker has stated requires either restating or paraphrasing essential aspects. It is possible for both sides to align their viewpoints and move on in a more successful manner by using this strategy, which helps explain any misunderstandings or ambiguities that may have arisen throughout the talk.

A third benefit of summarizing is that it indicates active participation and invites the speaker to expound more on their views. Active listening is a strong method that encourages the speaker to elaborate on their ideas and emotions. One such strategy is the use of open-ended questions. When compared to closed-ended questions, which are designed to elicit brief, factual replies, open-ended questions encourage more in-depth thinking and elaboration, so encouraging more meaningful discourse and the exploration of potential ideas. Through the use of open-ended questions, listeners will exhibit their real interest in comprehending the viewpoint of the speaker, which will, in turn, motivate them to express themselves in a more comprehensive manner.

What Bible has to say About Listening?

<u>Jesus and the Samaritan Woman:</u> In the encounter between Jesus and the Samaritan woman at the well, we see a beautiful demonstration of Jesus' ability to listen with respect and empathy, leading to a profound transformation. Firstly, Jesus defies social norms by engaging in conversation with a Samaritan woman, breaking down barriers of ethnicity, gender, and religion. Despite societal expectations, Jesus treats her with dignity and respect, recognizing her as a person worthy of attention and care.

Secondly, Jesus listens attentively to the woman's words and acknowledges her perspective. He shows empathy by understanding her situation and addressing her deepest needs. When Jesus speaks of living water, he taps into her spiritual thirst, demonstrating his understanding of her longing for something more meaningful in life.

Thirdly, Jesus doesn't judge or condemn the woman for her past. Instead, he gently guides her towards a deeper understanding of herself and of God. By revealing her past and present circumstances, Jesus shows her that he knows her fully yet still accepts her unconditionally.

Lastly, Jesus' genuine interest and compassion lead to a transformative encounter. The woman's encounter with Jesus at the well leaves her deeply moved and transformed. She becomes a witness, proclaiming Jesus as the Messiah to her community, leading many to believe.

In summary, Jesus' kind and sympathetic listening creates a secure environment in which the Samaritan lady may open up, sparking a deep discussion that changes both her life and the lives of many. This exchange exemplifies Jesus' extraordinary capacity to establish a personal connection with individuals from all backgrounds and socioeconomic classes.

<u>Moses and Jethro:</u> The conversation that Moses had with his biological father A profound lesson about the necessity of listening to sound advice and delegating poor leadership is provided by Jethro in Exodus 18; this lesson is very important. In the desert, Jethro pays a visit to Moses, and throughout his time there, he witnesses the great duty that Moses has of ruling the people from sunrise to dusk. Jethro is aware that this amount of labor cannot be maintained, and he suggests to Moses that he ought to assign the responsibility of deciding less significant concerns to more skilled leaders among the Israelites and that he should save himself for the most challenging situations. When Moses hears Jethro's counsel, he pays close attention to it because he recognizes its wisdom and practicability. This demonstrates his humility and willingness to learn from others despite the fact that he occupies the position of spiritual and political authority among the Israelites. He takes Jethro's advice without any reservations.

Moses not only alleviates his personal load by putting Jethro's advice into action, but he also inspires confidence in the community's leaders and gives them more authority for themselves. The Israelites develop a feeling of shared ownership and accountability as a result of this transfer of authority, which ultimately results in more effective government and more communal cohesiveness. Furthermore, the fact that Moses was prepared to listen to Jethro's counsel shows the significance of seeking guidance and assistance in times of need, especially for those who are in positions of authority. Moses, rather of obstinately insisting on doing everything alone, accepts aid with humility and learns from the knowledge of others, which eventually results in his being a more successful leader and averting burnout.

Biloxi Management Pearl: Be helpful. When you see a person without a smile, give him/her yours.

Scripture: *"Let each of you look not only to his own interests but also to the interests of others." **(Philippians 2:4)***

Application of Biloxi Management Pearl to the Lesson:

Personal Observation:

Yes, I pride myself on this one. I have various sayings and quotes that I have used and still use that have benefited me over the years. The oldest by far that started me on my smiling or grinning ways, as my Aunt Rose will say, comes from Ziggy, the comic strip character, probably some 45-50 years ago. "Keep a smile on your face; it makes everyone else wonder what you have been up to" This and this infectious laugh that I have been told that I have is from God. If I can bring a smile or laughter to someone else, then I have done my job.

Another one that I tend to use quite often is, "I believe that that work should be fun, and I am going to do my best to keep it that way." Yes, another is your smile will brighten up a cloudy day. The last is an oldie but a goodie, "Smile, you are on Candid Camera. If the old saying that smiling is contagious and smiling will cost you nothing, Lest we forget, one of the best things that we can give anyone is a smile, because it will brighten up their day and it will brighten up a cloudy day. It will cost you nothing, but the benefits are enormous, and it will inject a little humor, spread a little love, and lead to some friendship.

As a child growing up, I always kept a smile on my face. I remember in grade school; a teacher asked me what was wrong with my voice; it sounded like something was growling and trying to get out. So, I started to talk less and smile more, keep my mouth shut, if you will. However, I would soon train myself to laugh at will. It was easy for me, just think about something funny and make it 10 times funnier in my head; I could go from a smile to full laughter in no time flat. I knew it drove my mother crazy, as well as other adults.

I must admit, Life was so much fun back then; my siblings and I used to tell stories to entertain ourselves. Remember, we did not have cable (satellite and all-day and all-night television). Back then, in our city, there were just 3 television stations and the AM radio. Laughing came naturally to us; all we had was each other.

As a young supervisor/manager, I dared not smile too much. Back then, I did not smile, mainly because, in certain circles, it was frowned upon, viewed, and seen as a sign of weakness or incompetence. We always had this saying back then: we had 2 strikes against us already; we were young and black. We cannot afford to get the 3rd strike. However, as I grew older and more sure or confident in myself, I started to smile more; I no longer cared about how they or others viewed me. I started to miss what made

George, George. I started to look at the fun side of work, for the most part, anyway. It was around this time when I started to use the saying more, that work should be fun, and I am going to do my best to keep it that way.

The tables have turned. I learned that instead of holding back my smile, I started to give people, co-workers, and total strangers my smile, my laughter. Soon, they too started to see that you/I can be a good, effective supervisor/manager and still have fun in the process. I didn't have to trade in my smile for a frown in order not to show that it was a weakness or of fear of being viewed as incompetent.

Have you ever worked in a place where you were afraid to talk or laugh? Maybe even a supervisor/manager who either did not know how or was afraid to smile. Sourpuss is what they were called, if my mind serves me correctly. I can imagine that it was a boring job, and the hours were even longer, almost like working in a tomb. Work is already hard and sometimes stressful enough without a supervisor/manager who is afraid or doesn't want to smile. Help lighten the load, share the burden, and lighten up the room. Better yet, if you see someone without a smile, give them yours. For one thing, there are a lot more where that one came from, and there is no shortage of them. Above all, they are free, just for the asking.

Now go out there and keep smiling, and smiling, and smiling!!!

Biloxi Management Pearl: "Ability is what you're capable of doing.

Motivation determines what you do.

Attitude determines how well you do it." Lou Holtz

Scripture:" The fear of the Lord is the beginning of wisdom; all those who practice it have a good understanding. His praise endures forever!" (Psalm 111:10)

Application of Biloxi Management Pearl to the Lesson:

Personal Observation:

I have used a variation of this as a more seasoned supervisor/manager. I used this because I believe that I did not have supervisory/managers in the true sense of the word. I had mentors, or those who sought to instill in me values, these values helped mold me (among other things and other people, of course) and helped me to become the supervisor/manager that I became in my later years. These things that I hoped to have passed on to a younger generation.

Please don't misunderstand me. I had my share of bad or poor supervisors/managers, too, but even with them, they taught me, or I learned something from them in their actions or inactions, if you will. Those who trusted my judgment and my abilities, I will speak of first. We all have unique abilities; it may be in some areas where we are better than in other areas. Therefore, we can do a lot of things; the question is how well it is. A good supervisor/manager will help you to see and focus on your abilities and not only get you to see that you are more than just capable of doing it, but you are quite capable and efficient in doing it, as well. Basically, you are not only capable of doing the task, but you are confident in your ability. It is one thing to be capable; it is a whole different thing or level to be confident in your ability.

I remember when I was a lot younger, my supervisor showed that confidence in me, TK would always say George, it's yours, "handle it, handle it", and then she would walk away. That in and of itself gave me the confidence knowing that 1. she trusted me and my judgment and 2. if I had a question, she was there to help. If I made a mistake, she would come to my cubicle, sit down, and we would discuss it. To me a mentor to a mentee, this is how you, I learned and grew, as a leader.

Motivation determines what you do. Think about that for a while: if you have the ability and the capability to do the task and someone gives you the confidence to move forward, that is, in essence, trust in you as a person. This confidence to move forward is the cog in the wheel that gives you the motivation or the drive, if you will, to do the task. Trust breeds trust, and mistrust breeds mistrust. If your supervisor gives you a task or an assignment with little direction or no oversight, he or she is saying one of two things. One is I trust in you and your abilities; I believe you can complete this assignment. The other is I don't trust in you and your abilities; I believe you are incapable of completing this assignment. Either way, it is up to you to prove them right or wrong. I remember seeing a quote from Stephen Curry of the Golden State Warriors, that went something like, "Just don't prove others wrong; prove to yourself that you are right."

When you complete the assigned task on time and correct, with very few or any changes by the supervisor, that shows they have confidence in you, that you did it correctly and that you have proven them right in the same vein, placed yourself in the right spot, going forward. If they did not believe you were capable, you have now shown them that they /he/she were wrong about you and that you were up to the task.

Now, instead of being a team member, when you look at those persons you supervise, not as subordinates but as team members, this fosters a sense of belonging to something greater than themselves or synergy, if you will. When this is done and done correctly, you, as the supervisor should be preparing your team members to move up in the organization, or maybe a promotion. When ready, you should invite them to apply for certain positions, or at the very least, you should ask them think about applying for the position. By requesting that they apply for certain positions show that you are confident in their abilities, this in turn should be motivation that they are ready to move up and take on more responsibilities, for growth.

Attitude determines how well you do it. In a nutshell or simply speaking, your motivation or drive on the assigned task determines how well you do it. Are you engaged in the project? Are you actively seeking out opportunities? It has been said that success is where opportunity meets preparation. All because you have the ability and you received the confidence. Also, remember that opportunity only knocks once.

If that opportunity only knocks once, remember to pray for guidance and that it is for you and that it is God's will for you. That way when opportunity comes knocking, you have already prayed about it and developed the ability that you are capable and confident. This confidence (not arrogance) has given you the determination and the attitude to accept his will for you. Now, not only are you waiting for the knock to come, but you are expecting it, for it is our Lord and Savior, Jesus Christ, with good news for you and your new endeavors.

Now, Go for it!!!!

Biloxi Management Pearl: "If your actions inspire others to dream more, learn more, do more and become more, you are a leader." John Quincy Adams

Scripture: *"In everything, set them an example by doing what is good. In your teaching, show integrity, seriousness and soundness of speech that cannot be condemned so that those who oppose you may be ashamed because they have nothing bad to say about us." (**Titus 2:7-8**)*

Application of Biloxi Management Pearl to the Lesson:

Personal Observation:

Dare to Dream

If this is the case, then my days as an adjunct would be a good example. I guess my team members and others always said and meant it. George, "I want to be just like you" when I grow up.

They always told me how they kept my emails when I replied to a question professionally yet firmly and to the point. Quoting regulation when and if needed. Always having their back when needed. Encouraging them and coaching them when appropriate.

In my younger years as a supervisor/manager, they were my employees. In my later years, they became my team members.

Yes, I was accused of being hardheaded and refusing to give in when questioned, but my reply was always the same: "If I am the leader of this team and I must answer for the actions of this team, I can answer and respond appropriately only if I did the action.

If I listen to you and change my mind just because you want me to, then you would be the leader and not me. At the very least, you would lose respect for me as the leader of the team because I appeared to be wishy-washy or unsure of myself. Plus, if I did, would you stop there, and would you respect me as the leader of this team? Normally, the answer, after thinking about it, would be "No".

My all-time favorite would be, you have about 5 minutes to change my mind; use it wisely. After about 2 ½ minutes (to change my mind) after the 2 ½ minutes, my mind would be half-closed. Everything after 5 minutes, and all I will hear is gibberish, at best. My mind would be made up. I did this so as to not waste time with idle talk for 5-10 minutes or more. Think about what is important and why your way is better. I am not saying that I am perfect, but I put a lot of thought into my decisions, and "because I think it is better "is not going to move the needle in changing my mind. How is your proposed decision better for the project and/or department."

It is good to have an open mind. However, it's even better to know when to close it.

It is Christmas time in the city; literally, it is Christmas time as I write this. I am reminded of the movie "It's "A Wonderful Life". I have seen parts of this movie, but I have never really taken the time to really see the movie. We are all leaders in our own right. As I was conducting a Session under VU, I had a captive audience, and I told them (plus it was my birthday, so I was talkative) I told them, among other things, during the break, that we may never know just how far-reaching our words go. A kind word here and a helping hand there will go a long way. Sometimes, things we tell or do (Actions) to a person may cogitate for days, hours, weeks, maybe even months or years, before what you said comes full circle. You have inspired that person into greatness, or somewhere, a place they thought they would never go or ever be. All because of what you said or did weeks, months or years ago.

We think in terms of now. We think that we must inspire people now to be leaders, which is a big misconception, in my opinion. Have you ever thought why they have the saying, "If you can read this, thank a teacher"? They have great influence over the minds of tomorrow.

Next to our family, who has a great deal of influence in our lives, there are others. When I speak of family, I am not necessarily talking about family as it relates to blood or kinship. As stated, earlier; teachers shape the minds of tomorrow. If you want to read something funny, we are ALL teachers. Our words and actions are not for children and adults either. Other adults can learn from adults, and adults can learn from children. If you think I am joking, just listen and watch the innocence of a young child. Their actions make us want to be better.

Remember that person from school that you thought would make a terrible parent and ended up being a very good one? We never know how far-reaching our words and actions will impact others, either directly or indirectly.

How indirectly, you ask? Sometimes, things that we say and do will change a person's disposition, and that will, in turn, change the people around them to want to do better and be better. Remember, it is not always about you, I, we, and us.

Now, back to "It's a Wonderful Life," I believe that we all have guardian angels; just because we don't see them, it does not mean they are not there. God supplies us with all our needs. The second point is that we will never know how this world would be if you, we, and I were not in it. In the movie, the lead character saved his brother when he was young; if he had not been there to save is brother, his brother would not have been there to save the people that he did save later in life. Basically, the words and actions inspired others, if you had not been here to do it, this world would be different.

I will end this, which is a saying on my birthday every year: Today, on this day, some xx years ago, my mother, Mary E. (Honey) Humphrey, would bring forth her fourth child and his name would be George Anthony Humphrey, and the world has not been the same since. Because of each one of you who are reading this book and all my friends and acquaintances throughout my lifetime, I can truthfully say the same thing about you because since you came into this world, it has not been the same, and just by knowing you, I have not been the same since.

Biloxi Management Pearl: "Lack of direction, not lack of time. We all have twenty-four-hour days." Zig Ziglar, *Little Book of Big Quotes*

Scripture: "Woe to the world because of its stumbling blocks! For it is inevitable that stumbling blocks come, but woe to that man through whom the stumbling block comes!" (Matthew 18:7)

Application of Biloxi Management Pearl to the Lesson:

Personal Observation:

I have truly been blessed. In my lifetime, I have read many books. Back when we were children, we only had 3 television stations and the AM radio stations. Oh, how times have changed. That was not much to keep active boys busy. Sitting and looking at the four walls would not cut it, and TV and AM radio did not offer much. Playing outside was good, and reading a good book, even back then, was fun and sometimes entertaining. So, as I grew older, I continued to enjoy reading. Now during my lifetime and of all the books I have read, there are several that have influenced my role as a supervisor/manager. These books have gone a long way in shaping me as a supervisor/manager.

One book was required reading, *Six Thinking Hats* by de Bono. This book, as stated earlier, required reading while working on my doctorate, so I really don't like to count that because there were many others. However, this one stood out above the rest. The first book, I believe, was published in 1990, entitled *"We Have Got to Start Meeting Like This: A Guide to Successful Meeting Management"* By Mosvick & Nelson.

Although both books are good, the book "We Have Got to Start Meeting Like This: A Guide to Successful Meeting Management" was better, mainly because it is a book that I wanted to read. The book is very good in that it helped me to organize my meetings at work and manage my projects a lot better and more efficiently. I believe these books helped me to become a better supervisor/manager. I also decided to use some of it in my personal life, as well.

These two books allowed me to realize more than others on this management pearl. It is true; each one of us is given 24 hours in a day. All the money and gold in the world cannot buy you one day or one minute more.

When we really think about it, we do not need more time; we need more focus and more direction. What do we do with our /your 24 hours? What I have learned, first from the meeting book, in my opinion, is invaluable. I found myself timing myself on how long it would take me to do a project, walk a distance, read a story etc. I then was able to gauge how long and how much I could do based on what my "to-do" list looks like. It has worked wonders for me when I am on a short deadline. I can prioritize the time and tasks that I do have. I have even built on or added to more times for things that may unexpectedly come up. If I finish early or sooner than expected, I either go to the next item on my to-do list or reward myself and take a short break before going on to the next project on hand.

The Bono book, No, I did not forget about this one. However, this book taught me, or I learned, if you will, to be more critical of myself and my work. No, I don't use all the thinking hats, but I will use several of them, depending on the circumstances and the subject at hand. Has it made me a better person, supervisor/manager, I believe so. I have learned over the years that, especially in my work life, people appreciate it when you state what you are going to do, how long it is going to take and how long it will take. It allows them to manage their time more wisely. Even if it (meeting, project, etc.) goes over the allotted time, we can be flexible to table it until later if need be.

In my personal/private life, well, let's just say I am happy with myself. For a child who always received U's (Unsatisfactory) in grade school in "using self-control," I am pretty good at it now.

Back in the day, we received report cards, and on the back, we received an S-Satisfactory or U-Unsatisfactory from our teacher. Well, let's just say that my letter grades were pretty good; overall, I probably could have been better if I had mastered "using self-control" and "using time wisely." Well, according to my teachers at that time anyway, so they say, I just could not get past those U's.

Hey, I could not be good at everything, could I?

Biloxi Management Pearl: "Life is simply too short to be so little." Prof. C. David Loeks (UPI & SU, c. 1986)

Scripture: "The fear of the Lord is instruction in wisdom, and humility comes before honor." (Proverbs 15:33)

Application of Biloxi Management Pearl to the Lesson:

Personal Observation:

Life is short, and when you really think about it, it is so little. Life is short, and yet, life is long; it is simple and yet complex; it is all we want, yet it is nothing we want. The more we have, the more we want. The fewer we have, the fewer we want. We are not satisfied, yet we are comfortable.

First, life is short and little. I believe the longest years are between the time we are born and the time we turn twenty. Give or take. The longest 12 years are between 1st grade and 12th grade or high school graduation. We learn a lot of things during those formative years. We then learn to hone those skills during the next 20-30 years. **Proverbs 22:6** - Train up a child in the way he should go: and when he is old, he will not depart from it. **Ephesians 6:4** - And ye fathers provoke not your children to wrath: but bring them up in the nurture and admonition of the Lord. **Proverbs 29:15** - The rod and reproof give wisdom: but a child left [to himself] bringeth his mother to shame. Then, in our later years, we learn to compensate for the rest of the years we have on this earth. We now understand the true meaning of not bringing shame upon our families.

Normally, as we age, we learn to become more spiritual/religious. We start to understand death and our own mortality the best we can, anyway. We start to understand when our parents used to tell us, "There are just as many short graves in the cemeteries as there are long ones." When we are young, we don't quite understand what is being said, but we will come to understand it little by and by. Now, for those of us who have lost a loved one through the sting of death, it brings about a whole new meaning. The closer we are to the person during life, the harder it is to accept their death/departure/transition. We find ourselves reminiscing and thinking about the person. We think about their wise sayings, their laughter, their smile, their fellowship, friendship and kinship. We come full circle and realize how short and precious life really is.

Life is short and yet life is long. Every day is a blessing. Even if we live to be 100, it is still short. Yet we must remember the saying it is not about how many years we have in this life, but how much life we have in those years. Yet, if we live our lives with Godly wisdom and don't worry about the years of life, but instead the life in those years that we do have left, it will lead to a richer, more fulfilling life. I remember many, many years ago, I think it was Travis Smiley on the TJMS when he spoke of death as it is normally written on our obituary or tombstone, etc. Our whole life is captured in that dash between birth and death.

As I have heard it said, and I think it is a quote by Mark Twain, "Sing like no one is listening, love as you have never been hurt, dance like no one is watching and live like it is heaven on earth." These are words to remember and to live by.

Life is simple yet complex. I told my two sons when they were very young that life is nothing more than 3 C's (Choices, Chances and Consequences, thereof). Later it became CDC - Choices, Decisions, and the Consequences there of. If anybody tells you anything different, they are lying". We make decisions every day and every minute of the day and of our lives (for the most part). What to eat, when to eat, what time to get up, what time to go to the bathroom (yes, we do think this is a good movie, and I wonder if I can hold it for 5 more minutes). Also, the car and or house we purchase or the place we choose to live, people we become involved with and or marry. The chances are that everything will turn out right or can and will work out as planned because, yes, we do want a desired outcome. Finally, we learn the consequences of those actions or decisions, good, bad, or indifferent. Then, the cycle continues. Don't get me wrong, sometimes we make the correct decision, and unfortunately, when it comes to affairs of the heart, the other person realizes that they made the wrong decision.

I remember as a supervisor /manager I learned to depend on God on who to hire and when. I allowed him to lead me and allow him to guide me to those who needed my help and assistance. Remember, when in a supervisory position, we must be mindful of Who to coach, when to delegate and how to delegate. As the years went by, I learned **(Proverbs 3:5-6)** Trust in the Lord with all your heart and lean not on your own understanding; in all your ways acknowledge Him, and He shall direct your paths.

Yet, it is all we want, yet nothing we want. But, on our decisions (choices, chances, and consequences throughout our years on earth and as we live our time and lives and, of course, how we handle or deal with those consequences with more decisions and chances.) As we get older, we learn to trust, or we should learn to trust in God and have faith in Him and his will for us. Trust and allow him to guide your decision. Therefore, the chance of a bad decision is minimized, and the consequences are good. Even if the consequences are not good, it will help you to feel better about the consequences, knowing that he will deliver and be there for you, even to the end of time. In the end, you will feel better and come to learn and realize that life is too short to be so little.

Trust Him.

Biloxi Management Pearl: A right move is never wrong; a wrong move is never right.

Scripture: *"Be careful with nothing, but in everything by prayer and supplication with thanksgiving let your requests be made known unto God." **(Philippians 4:6)***

Application of Biloxi Management Pearl to the Lesson:

Personal Observation:

A wise man/person once said that a fool hesitates, and a wise man thinks things over or there about. It took me a long time to understand what it meant, being a child at the time; it would take a few years for it to sink in and take the time to determine what you want to do, in general, in life, etc...Pray about it, plan your steps wisely, trust God and have Faith that God will guide your steps, and make the move with faith and confidence. The more faith you have, the more you plan, and the more confidence you have will greatly determine if the move is the right move.

Pray and allow the Spirit of the Lord to move you. If so, even if it is the wrong move for you (or so you believe), it is the right move for God. He will, in turn, make it the right move. In the Book of **(Proverbs 3:5)**, you will see this: "Trust in the LORD with all your heart and lean not on your own understanding;"

However, if you fail to plan, fail to believe, fail to trust God and believe in **(Proverbs 3:5)** and fail to move with confidence, you will soon find out that you have made a wrong move. A wrong move is never right, and a right move is never wrong. If you do not believe in God and trust and have faith that he alone can and will lead you and direct your path.

I remember one time as a young supervisor/manager; I had a saying that I like to use, "If you are good and you know that you are good (not in an arrogant or cocky sense), Let me repeat myself, when you are good and you know that you are good, there is nothing to worry and you don't have to say a word, your actions will speak for itself and it is just a matter of time before others realize it for themselves.

This one was born from my mother, in that as a young man, when we were getting ready for an event, church, etc., I would be all dressed up and looking good (Even, if I have to say so myself.) I would look at my mom and ask, Hon (My Mother's name is Mary E. (Honey) Humphrey, and of course, her nickname was Honey). I look good, don't I? She would look at me and reply, "You look like George." I would look at her and ask the question a different way, "But George looks good, right? Her reply would be, "You look like George". This went on for years, even until my adulthood and her death (She never did give me the answer I wanted, though).   I really miss that short, meaningful conversation, as I hope my sons will one day miss them with me. I miss them so, not only because of this particular conversation, but many others, as well. She taught me humility/humbleness and that I did not need anybody's validation because I am a child of God, and I already know how good I am (and how good I look to, well back then anyways).

In essence, when you feel good about a move or doing something, be it as a supervisor/manager or just in your everyday walk, you know it is a good move because you can feel it. It can be a good deed for someone else or about a purchase. You have thought about it, prayed about it. **(James 1:5)**

"If any of you lack wisdom, let him ask of God, that giveth to all *men* liberally, and up braideth not; and it shall be given him." Now you have that confidence, that swagger that only the good Lord himself can place on your heart. That is when you make your move, and it will be the right move.

Remember, don't make your move too soon, though, by listening to others and not God himself because they will fool you. The devil is always around, trying to lead you astray.

You have now made your move, sometimes, despite what others are saying or telling you what you should do. Don't take that job, it is too hard for you, don't marry that person, he /she is not good for you, don't buy that piece of clothing, it does not look good on you.

Ultimately, making the right move is about decision-making and the decision-making process and skills that come with it. If you are truly listening and you follow **(Philippians 4:6)**. If you are truly listening, you will know that a right move is never wrong, and a wrong move is never right. Why, you ask, because the prophet Isaiah says so in **(Isaiah 30:21)**: "And thine ears shall hear a word behind thee, saying, this *is* the way, walk ye in it, when ye turn to the right hand, and when ye turn to the left."

Biloxi Management Pearl: It doesn't matter which side of the fence you get off on. What matters most is getting off. You cannot make progress without making decisions.

Scripture: "No one can serve two masters, for either he will hate the one and love the other, or he will be devoted to the one and despise the other. You cannot serve God and money." (Matthew 6:24)

Application of Biloxi Management Pearl to the Lesson:

Personal Observation:

This is an excellent follow-up to the preceding Management Pearl ("Life is simply too short to be so little." Prof. C. David Loeks (UPI & SU, c. 1986)). Leaders must be decisive, make a stand, commit to the left or to the right. Whether you are right (correct) or wrong (incorrect) will not make that big of a difference if the decision is well-grounded in facts, as you know of it, at that time anyway.

No one likes an indecisive or wishy-washy leader, a leader who has the backbone of over-cooked pasta, a leader who goes the way the wind blows. However, an indecisive leader or wishy-washy leader is better than no decision at all. Please note that an indecisive leader goes to and or toward an uncommitted decision. At a minimum, or at the least, it will allow you to move forward in your work, and everyone is going in the same direction. Basically, you have direction; it may be the wrong direction, but at least there is movement, and everyone is moving in the same direction.

A leader who does not make a decision will not progress or move or come to realize the team's potential. Basically, here, there is no movement; we have stagnation. Even worse, everyone is going in their own direction. Chaos ensues, and first, to correct it, you must stop everyone, then regroup and then start moving forward; it is just a thing or turning that juggernaut around and getting back on track, no matter how long it may take.

Bear in mind, that every decision you make will not be the right decision because we will not always have the information to make the right decision at our fingertips. The best we can do is if we cannot make the right decisions to make the most optimal decision we can with the information we have available at that time.

Once the decision is made, stick to your guns, and try not to be swayed or influenced by others and what others tell you about what they would do if they were you and what you should do. Unless, of course, they bring new facts that you did not have before. No one really knows what they would do in any given circumstance until they are in the circumstance, of course. Unless you have pre-planned for the circumstance if it arose, keeping it realistic, at that point, it is a planned action, makes sense?

Remember, when all is said and done, you will have to answer to the decision you made. Only you can adequately explain WHY YOU MADE THE DECISION YOU DID. If that is the case, you might as well let it be yours.

Also, when in doubt about a decision, follow your heart, your gut instincts, and your first mind. Follow your training, experience, and education, and listen and follow God, and not necessarily in that order. If you listen and pray that God will lead you in the decision, he will.

Don't be pressured to make a decision, especially a quick decision, unless it is a life and death matter. Remember, sometimes God is trying to tell you something, if you will only listen. God is God all by himself; He can make a way out of no way. If you trust him, seek Him out and believe in Him. If you do, you will realize that even if you make the wrong decision, you can make it right.

Just believe, trust, and have Faith.

Biloxi Management Pearl: "Whenever you are asked if you can do a job, tell 'me, 'Certainly I CAN!' – and get busy and find out how to do it." Theodore Roosevelt, 26th U.S. President

Scripture: "And not only this, but we also exult in our tribulations, knowing that tribulation brings about perseverance; and perseverance, proven character; and proven character, hope; and hope does not disappoint because the love of God has been poured out within our hearts through the Holy Spirit who was given to us." (Romans 5:3-5)

Application of Biloxi Management Pearl to the Lesson:

Personal Observation:

Never pass up a chance to show others how good you are and how good your God is. Usually, when someone in a management or leadership position asks you to do something, it is because they have confidence in your work and or because they see something in you, potential as it were, that needs to be brought to the forefront. They are, in essence, saying I trust and believe that you can do this. I have confidence in your abilities. All you must do is show them that they are correct.

During your lifetime, you may have heard someone say, or you may have said, "I wouldn't want your job." One thing I have heard is that "the can't, never can." Branch out, Trust God and believe; you will soon come to realize that it is not that difficult. In a leadership role, much like life, there is nothing new under the sun, nothing you probably have not seen and or experienced or at least read about or saw before. The difference is that it comes wrapped in a different package with different words, symbols, etc.

I remember taking a woodworking night class in my younger days, more as a hobby than anything else. What I learned from that class was priceless. I will never look at a piece of furniture or anything made of wood the same way. I find myself, or I found myself looking at certain things, such as tables and chairs, etc. They were nothing more than other pieces of wood, joined together by glue, nails, staples, etc., until we got to the finished product.

Unwrap the package. Once you unwrap the package and understand the words and symbols, you will already have the answer. Remember, new challenges bring about or bring on new and more responsibilities and that in and of itself helps us to grow and become who God wants us to be, in his perfect will. So, when a new assignment comes your way, break the cycle of never going outside your comfort zone. I tried it, and yes, it was hard, but it was also very rewarding and, yes, very challenging. However, above all, it allowed me to grow as a person and as a manager/supervisor.

Keep in mind if you always go where you have always gone, you will always be where you have always been. If you always do what you have always done, you will always get what you already have.

Trust God, break the cycle and see what He has waiting on you outside of the cycle. Remember, this cycle does not have to be a job or position; it can come in many forms: Job, romance, love life, etc. If you are having the same problems with the same people or the people you meet, it may not be them; it may be you. Start looking to attract and mingle with another type of people, the reward will be yours.

Biloxi Management Pearl: "A pessimist is one who makes difficulties of his opportunities, and an optimist is one who makes opportunities of his difficulties." Harry Truman

Scripture: *"See then that ye walk circumspectly, not as fools, but as wise, Redeeming the time, because the days are evil. Wherefore be ye not unwise, but understanding what the will of the Lord is. And be not drunk with wine, wherein is excess; but be filled with the Spirit; Speaking to yourselves in psalms and hymns and spiritual songs, singing and making melody in your heart to the Lord; Giving thanks always for all things unto God and the Father in the name of our Lord Jesus Christ;"* ***(Ephesians 5:15-20 KJV).***

Application of Biloxi Management Pearl to the Lesson:

Personal Observation:

This is a twist on if the glass is half full or half empty. A pessimist is a person who is given an opportunity to move up or showcase his /her talents but instead bemoans the opportunity. I am doing the supervisor's work; I am not going to do his/her work for him. I am not getting paid to do that. These are all pessimistic attitudes and sayings. I am not saying that it is right or wrong; it is just the wrong attitude.

Think about it, even if you are doing the supervisor's work, so what? If you do it and do it correctly, you are demonstrating to your supervisor, and your higher leadership, not to mention yourself, that you are willing, able, and capable of being a leader/supervisor in the organization. Also, you can put this in your resume when you decide to leave the organization.

I have a saying that I have used throughout my career, "If you are good and you know that you are good. Let me repeat this; if you are good and you know that you are good (not in a cocky or arrogant sense, but more in a candid as that of being confident in your abilities), you don't have to tell anyone about it, it is just a matter of time before they realize it for themselves."

Now, on the other hand, or on the flip side of that an optimist is a person who will take on whatever assignment that is given and see it as a challenge instead of a hindrance or roadblock. One does not worry about what or who will receive the credit; if the job is done, the mission is completed, and it is done correctly and on time.

Please, don't get me wrong; at one point (especially when I was a younger supervisor/manager), I was concerned about who would get the credit and not doing my supervisor's work. Then, I had to remember to trust God, and all will work out according to His perfect will. All you must do is be obedient and trust him and don't worry about who will get the credit. For the credit always goes to God Himself.

Because when you really think about it, to God goes all the credit for everything good in this life and to God, be the Glory.

Biloxi Management Pearl: "The reward of suffering is experience." Harry Truman

*Scripture: "And not only so, but we glory in tribulations also: knowing that tribulation worketh patience; And patience, experience; and experience, hope." **(Romans 5:3-4)***

Application of Biloxi Management Pearl to the Lesson:

Personal Observation:

Jesus has been referred to as the suffering servant. Servant, I believe, was the name of one of our Sunday School Lessons. Life has its peaks and valleys, the good and the bad, and, of course, all the in-between.

I remember reading a billboard a long time ago that changed my life forevermore ever since. I am paraphrasing now, of course; the sign reads the bad things in life are meant to make us better, not bitter. I have seen and read it many times since then, but that was my first time. It was the time that it spoke to me when I needed it most.

Changing me, I came to realize and understand the saying that this, too, will come to pass. We must go through our going through, as Pastor Canada would say. We must go through the storms and bitter things in life; we must experience the sting of death in our lives. We must suffer to get the experience we need to move forward.

As we suffer, we gain the experience that God is with us. We weather through the storms of life and when things are not going well on the job, at home, with the children, etc. When work got too hard, I learned not to trust in my own understanding; it was an experience for me both for my work as well, my job and my future endeavors, but most importantly, to continue to trust in God.

As I write this, I am reminded of a poem, Footprints, that I still love to read, especially the end of it. In the poem Footprints, in the sand and as I look back over my life and I see one set of footprints in the sand, I knew it was then that he carried me. Now, I am stronger and more confident in my going through based on the suffering I had to endure.

However, I do know this: 1. My suffering is nothing compared to the suffering that He, Jesus, endured. 2. Whatever life may bring me; I know we can handle it together. 3. It is good to know that when I get tired or weak, He will be there to carry me, just like He always has.

Go ahead and gain that experience.

Biloxi Management Pearl: "It is amazing what you can accomplish if you do not care who gets the credit." Harry Truman

Scripture: *"And let us not grow weary of doing good, for in due season we will reap if we do not give up." **(Galatians 6:9)***

Application of Biloxi Management Pearl to the Lesson:

Personal Observation:

Is being young problematic in and of itself? The problem when we were young, me included, back then was that we wanted to be recognized; we wanted to feel good about ourselves and get our name out there. We want our supervisors and co-workers to know how smart we are, how intelligent and how good we are. So, we sacrifice our creative juices, if you will, because we don't want anyone to take credit for our ideas. Selfish, yes, we want to get ahead, you bet. Do we care about what we can accomplish if we were not so selfish, not a bit.

As I stated earlier, when I was fresh out of college, yes, that was me. I was more concerned about myself and making a name for myself, the organization, and the people I served.

As I grew older, I started to realize how much I could accomplish and how much I did accomplish. This is also around the same time when I first started using my favorite quote: if you are good and you know that you are good, you don't have to tell anyone about it, and it is just a matter of time before they come to realize it for themselves.

I started to become more self-confident. I no longer cared about who received the credit. As a matter of fact, I got to the point that I wanted to float just below the radar, as I would say, back then. I did not want to bring attention to myself. I had now become just the opposite of the person I was years earlier. Now, when a supervisor asks me to do something, not only do I do it, but I also explain to my supervisor how I came to the conclusion I came to. This allowed my supervisor to know what I did; how I did it and the rationale for doing it that way. Just in case their superiors wanted to know how he arrived at that conclusion on the report. Yes, you read it correctly, the rationale, not my rationale for doing that way. I had come full circle in that I no longer cared who got the credit.

In essence, I had freed myself from the chains that had me bound. I was now grateful for the opportunity to show what I knew, my God-given talents. Now instead of hiding it, I showcased it for others to learn from what I knew. I now had no fear of anyone stealing my ideas.

I am grateful, free, and happy and am no longer concerned or care about who gets the credit. Helping others is more satisfying.

Try it! You may come to enjoy it.

Biloxi Management Pearl: "Things turn out best for those who make the best out of the way things turn out…" Art Linkletter

Scripture: "For our light affliction, which is but for a moment, worketh for us a far more exceeding and eternal weight of glory." (2 Corinthians 4:17)

Application of Biloxi Management Pearl to the Lesson:

Personal Observation:

I know it sounds like an oxymoron. However, it is all about how you see the land or view the world. No matter what life sends your way, you make the best of it. That adage, when life sends you lemons, you make lemonade.

Is it that easy? No, it is not that easy. Can you make it that easy? Well, of course, you can. The key is simple: Trust God that he will make a way. Believe in God's Holy word that if it is his will, it will come to pass. Believe in God; believe in yourself that you can do it and that all things are possible. The final step is really to step out on faith. Faith, according to the bible, **(Hebrews 11:1).** Now faith is the substance of things hoped for, the evidence of things not seen."

I remember growing up and hearing about making the best of a bad situation. As I grew older, I remember what it took and how I felt that no matter how things got in my life, there was nothing that God and I could not handle together.

So, no matter what you have gone through, what you are going through or what you may /will go through, it is true that everything will turn out best for those who make the best out of the way things turn out. So, remember, if you have breath in your body and God grants you another day, use that day to make things better. Not only that, but if you also try and make others feel better, you will soon find out that you are indeed making the best out of the way things turned out.

As I look back over my life, there were several times when I made the best of what was before me. I could not see a way out; I had no idea how I would make it through. But by the Grace of God, with all His grace and mercies, we made it through it.

On a different note, I came to realize that even in my belief, my situation did not get better, but it did make me feel better about the situation I was in.

Try God and See!!!

Biloxi Management Pearl: "The harder I work, the luckier I become." Lee Trevino

Scripture: *"Behold, happy is the man whom God correcteth: Therefore, despise not thou the chastening of the Almighty."*

(Job 5:17)

Application of Biloxi Management Pearl to the Lesson:

Personal Observation:

I remember hearing a saying that goes something like this: "Hard work pays off." Basically, if you work hard for the things in life that you want, you will achieve it. So, if you equate hard work with luck, then we are talking about an oxymoron. Allow me to explain that luck is defined as success or failure apparently brought on by chance rather than through one's own actions. Another one is that it is a force that brings good fortunes or that will cause things or good things to happen to you, again, by chance. So, it is possible that hard work is the force. However, if that is the case, we would have to determine and operationalize what is considered hard work as compared to just work. To look at it another way, if it happens by chance, it does not matter how we work; if we do nothing, not ever, etc., luck will come to us, whether work is involved or not.

Now, I must agree with our Sunday school leader, and others who believe this, and that is "I don't believe in luck" or "there is no such thing as luck". However, I do believe in the word. *"In the beginning was the Word, and the Word was with God, and the Word was God."* **(John 1:1)**.

If luck is by chance, and I don't believe that anything happens by chance, our good fortunes are a blessing, and our blessing comes from God.

Think that car, house, or job that you got or wanted and received is by luck or chance. That meeting with your significant other was not a chance meeting. Placed another way, your new mate, of casual encounter is not and was not luck or chance. That promotion or new job that you received or didn't receive, that near accident, that you missed by seconds and or minutes (or inches or feet). No, these things did not happen by chance or luck; these are blessings from God. So, enjoy your blessing and don't be afraid to tell others while you are at it. Not in an arrogant or holier than thou or in a case of bragging, of course. Then, pass that blessing on to someone else.

Always keep in mind that what someone else has is their blessing; be happy for them and their blessings. Yes, work hard, believe in God, and have faith and trust in God. "But let every man prove his own work, and then shall he have rejoicing in himself alone and not in another, for every man shall bear his own burden. Let him that is taught in the word communicate unto him that teaches in all good things. Be not deceived; God is not mocked:

for whatsoever a man soweth, that shall he also reap. **(Galatians 6:4-7).**

As supervisors/managers, we will, and we must always keep these words in mind. We must remember to do our best with and for those we work with. In the end you will get your own and just rewards.

Again, Trust and have Faith in God, Trust in his Holy word and believe there is nothing that can happen that He (God) and you cannot handle together!!

Why, you ask, the answer is simple, we must walk by Faith and not by sight.

Biloxi Management Pearl: "Talents are best nurtured in solitude, but character is best formed in the stormy billows of the world." Goethe

Scripture: "He that walketh righteously, and speaketh uprightly; he that despiseth the gain of oppressions, that shaketh his hands from holding of bribes, that stoppeth his ears from hearing of blood, and shutteth his eyes from seeing evil; He shall dwell on high: his place of defense shall be the munitions of rocks: bread shall be given him; his waters shall be sure." (Ephesians 2:8-9 KJV)

Application of Biloxi Management Pearl to the Lesson:

Personal Observation:

This is quite interesting, in those talents or autistic aptitude or general intelligence mental powers: ability: natural endowments of a person are best when we are alone or in solitude the place of being alone, but not lonely. It allows us to reflect on who we are and whose we are.

As a leader/supervisor/manager, these are our God-given traits, our DNA, what makes us and allows us to make the decisions we make. Yes, even supervisors/managers need some time to get away and refresh.

I remember as a young supervisor/manager how I pushed myself always trying to get better and be better at my job. Was I afraid to take time off? Maybe so? Not wanting to get left behind could be, or maybe just plain dedicated, possible.

I was, however, able to find myself and who I was when I started to check my own character. After all, our character is formed in the world. Our character, the way we think, behave, feel, our personality. Those things or attributes or features that make us different or distinguish us from all other people, those quirky idiosyncrasies that make us who we are and what other people love (or hate/dislike) about us. These are things/traits that we possess as a supervisors/manager or leadership traits that compel people to want to follow us.

Yes, we are a product of our environment, the world or our world view on things that have shaped and formed us into who we are and what we have become. As it has been said, when we learn better, we do better (or should, anyway). As my worldview started to change, I started to pay attention to those changes; I started to realize that no man is an island.

In my latter years as a supervisor/manager, I allowed God to have his way. I started to see things differently and, in my mind, my environment changed. When my environment changed, I changed. When I changed, I started to see more clearly what my purpose was. Remember, though, that this is not only as a supervisor/manager but as a person. Then, the true meaning of what it means when it is said, "When you learn better, you do better," started to sink in and become crystal clear. Yes, the lyrics (Amazing Grace), "I once was lost, but now am found, was blind, but now I see." is now crystal clear. All those days, those words that were lyrics in a song, and now, the meaning is there.

I know that I am not where I need to be, but I know I am a long way from where I used to be or where I was. These things that used to bother me no longer bother me. This tells me that I am better, and yes, I am moving in the right direction. I keep in mind **(Galatians 6:9),** "And let us not be weary in well doing: for in due season we shall reap if we faint not."

Biloxi Management Pearl: "Whatever you cannot understand, you cannot possess." Goethe

Scripture: "Be anxious for nothing, but in everything by prayer and supplication, with thanksgiving, let your requests be made known to God." (Philemon 4:6)

Application of Biloxi Management Pearl to the Lesson:

Personal Observation:

First, I am going to define a few terms like understand, possess, knowledge, power, and expand on a couple of them later. Why these terms, we must define, understand, and possess to get a basic understanding of what is being discussed. Knowledge, power, money, and wealth, because I believe these are the things that we covet. If we look at the term understand, which is to perceive the meaning of, grasp the idea of. Now, let's look at the word possess, which is to take for one's own or have as belonging to one. So basically, to have something, we must first perceive the meaning of grasp the idea of what we have. Knowledge, according to Merriam, is the fact or condition of knowing something with familiarity gained through experience or association.

If you possess power and knowledge, then you must understand the knowledge and power that you have.

Now, when you were a child, you understood the power and influence that your parents, adults, and authority figures had over you. As we grow older, we understand more and more how shallow that power really is. As a young supervisor/manager, I thought at that time, a few years out of college, that I had or possessed the knowledge, power, and understanding to be a great supervisor. I went straight by the book; I had the take-no-prisoner mentality. It was my way or the highway. My employees at the time hated it, but my superiors loved it. I made a name for myself in these circles; if they wanted something done and straightened out, get "George" on your team.

Ah, yes, I had the power until one day, I made a mistake; well, it really wasn't a mistake; it was a different opinion or viewpoint if you will. At that point everything started to change, and not for the better. Suddenly, I was the outsider; I had dared to question the status quo. Instead of being part of the solution, I was now a part of the problem. Yes, my eyes were opened, and yes, it was a most humbling experience.

In my life journey,

I have had friends, mentors, and supervisors who have taught me the true meaning of understanding and possessing power. Things can't always go by the book, and yes, there are extenuating circumstances. There is compassion, sympathy, empathy, and understanding; we are human beings with faults and shortcomings, and we are not perfect. Please, don't get me wrong, going by the book is good, but as supervisors/managers, we must learn and know when to use the book and when to pull out "The Book." "But be ye doers of the word, and not hearers only, deceiving your own selves." **(James 1:22)**. Thank you, God, for putting all the people in my life to help me understand the true meaning of power and knowledge and that it is you only who deserve the honor, praise and glory.

Now, go for it! I did and I now feel a lot better for doing so.

Understanding can be divided into distinct categories: The three dimensions are cognitive, emotional, and experiential. Cognitive comprehension encompasses the ability to logically and analytically grasp information, allowing individuals to effectively process data, solve problems, and make well-informed decisions. In situations that demand critical thinking and strategic planning, it is crucial. On the other hand, emotional understanding centers around empathy and the ability to recognize and acknowledge others' emotions. The ability to comprehend this type of information is essential for developing strong interpersonal relationships, creating a positive work environment, and efficiently managing team dynamics. Leaders who comprehend and effectively manage the emotions of their team members can significantly enhance morale and productivity. Experiential understanding is acquired by engaging in personal experiences and actively participating in practical activities. Enhancing individuals' ability to navigate complex situations and make sound judgments is facilitated by this type of understanding, which enables them to learn from both their successes and mistakes.

Additionally, hands-on experiences often offer deeper insights than theoretical knowledge alone, fostering resilience and adaptability.

Every type of understanding serves a distinct purpose in the realm of effective management. Strategic decision-making is aided by cognitive understanding, team cohesion and communication are improved by emotional understanding, and practical wisdom and adaptability are offered by experiential understanding. When combined, these approaches form a comprehensive framework for leadership that effectively tackles various challenges and opportunities in the workplace.

Possession: Possession involves more than just owning something; it also involves mastering it. Possessing knowledge extends beyond simply having information. It entails mastering that information and effectively applying it in various contexts. This level of mastery enables individuals to utilize their knowledge effectively in order to solve problems, foster innovation, and make well-informed decisions. Possessing power goes beyond simply holding a position of authority. It involves understanding how to effectively utilize that authority to inspire and lead others. A genuine leader utilizes their authority to inspire their team, foster constructive transformation, and accomplish shared objectives.

In both scenarios, the key to possession is the skillful and thoughtful utilization of one's possessions. Mastery of knowledge empowers individuals to transform ideas into actions and visions into reality, making it a powerful tool. When power is used wisely, it can foster an environment in which individuals feel valued, motivated, and aligned with the objectives of the organization. Possession, in its most comprehensive form, encompasses a profound comprehension and skillful utilization of one's possessions, be it knowledge, power, or any other resource. The concept of mastery transforms mere possession into a powerful force that can shape outcomes and propel success in different areas of life.

Biblical Context

<u>Philemon 4:6:</u> "I thank my God, making mention of thee always in my prayers, Hearing of thy love and faith, which thou hast toward the Lord Jesus, and toward all saints; That the communication of thy faith may become effectual by the acknowledging of every good thing which is in you in Christ Jesus."

(Philemon 4:6) encourages shifting from anxiety to faith through prayer, a change that can significantly empower managers. By adopting this mindset, managers can reduce stress and enhance their ability to make clear, compassionate decisions. When managers rely on faith, they cultivate a sense of inner peace and trust in the process, which helps them stay calm under pressure. This tranquility allows them to approach problems with a clear mind, making more thoughtful and effective decisions.

Moreover, incorporating prayer and gratitude into their daily routine can help managers maintain a positive outlook. Gratitude shifts focus from what's lacking to what's available, creating an environment of appreciation and optimism. Managers who express gratitude can inspire their teams, boost morale, and create a supportive and collaborative workplace culture.

A manager grounded in faith and gratitude is likely to be more empathetic, understanding, and patient with their team. This approach can lead to stronger relationships, better communication, and a more cohesive team. As a result, the workplace becomes a more positive and productive environment. In essence, the shift from anxiety to faith through prayer not only benefits managers personally but also positively impact their leadership and the overall work atmosphere.

Biloxi Management Pearl: "Nothing shows a man's character more than what he laughs at." Goethe

*Scripture: "And when ye see this, your heart shall rejoice, and your bones shall flourish like an herb: and the hand of the LORD shall be known toward his servants, and his indignation toward his enemies." **(Isaiah 66:14)***

Application of Biloxi Management Pearl to the Lesson:

Personal Observation:

Ah, yes. I learned this one a long time ago. As a fat kid growing up in Yazoo, MS, I started to laugh at myself. At first, it was a coping mechanism, and then I started to use it as a part of my everyday life. Now, very few people can say they have not seen me without a smile on my face or laughter in my heart.

Why? Do you ask that I have a character on the thing that I laugh at? To answer that question, let us first look at the definition of character. Merriam-Webster defines character as (among other things) the group of qualities that make a person, group, or thing different from others: A distinguishing feature. However, the one that I love is "the quality of being determined and able to deal with difficult situations." (Cambridge Dictionary)

As managers, leaders, and supervisors, we must know what to laugh at and when to laugh at it. We must realize that we cannot take everything seriously; we must be able to laugh at ourselves and with ourselves. We must understand that laughter truly is the best medicine. It allows us to be human, and it allows us to see, understand and take the appropriate action more adequately. When in a serious mood/situation, we think seriously about it; however, if you can find humor in the situation, you are more readily able to find a better solution. Basically speaking, it is hard to see or determine how you are going to get out of a problem/pickle until you first laugh at yourself for either getting in or allowing yourself to get into the problem to begin with.

Try it sometime. Sometimes, God may be trying to tell you something

Remember **(Ecclesiasticus 41:13)**: A good life hath but few days: but a good name endureth forever. So, laugh when you are happy or sad, when things are going your way and when they aren't. Those around you will also laugh, and laughter truly is the best medicine.

(Proverbs 17:22): A merry heart doeth good *like* a medicine: but a broken spirit drieth the bones.

So, go ahead, have fun, and enjoy life because God has you and by laughing, even when those who want to wish ill harm on you, will never know. In the process, you would have brought joy to a lot of people, and when people remember you, your good name and good nature will endure forever.

I will end this with a quote from A Christmas Carol miserly old Scrooge A Christmas Carol'. "There is nothing in the world so irresistibly contagious as laughter and good humor," the narrator says at the end.

Scrooge "became as good a friend, as good a master, and as good a man, as the good old city knew, or any other good old city...in the good old world." Now, go out and share your laughter and show your character.

Biloxi Management Pearl: "With great powers come great responsibilities." Uncle Ben (Spiderman 1)

Scripture: *"But he that knew not, and did commit things worthy of stripes, shall be beaten with few stripes. For unto whomsoever much is given, of him shall be much required: and to whom men have committed much, of him they will ask the more." **(Luke 12:48)***

Application of Biloxi Management Pearl to the Lesson:

Personal Observation:

I love this one, Spiderman 1, with Toby Maguire. When we supervise or if we are in any leadership position, we wield great powers from our superiors and the policy manual. With that comes the responsibility to do our best to the best of our abilities. Also, remember that authority can be delegated, but responsibility cannot.

We have a responsibility to our parents, husbands, wives, children, family, and friends and our fellowman and to God, to be the best that we can be. These are responsibilities that cannot and should not be taken lightly.

As we live on this great planet we call Earth, and only in this great nation we call the United States of America, we must realize that we have great power over this earth and this country, the best of ourselves. If God gave us dominion (Genesis) over all this planet and living creatures, we are doing a terrible job. We hear talk of Christian values, as though it is a club to beat someone on the head with. We want to control others with our rendition of Christian values instead of using those great powers to come to the table and discuss what is best, who knows we may have the same values, we just call it a different name. As that old saying goes, if it looks like a rose and smells like a rose, then it must be a rose.

However, I might like using the more generic name of the flower, but you will never know if you use your powers to beat in my head that it is a rose.

We have the power and responsibility to make the planet and this nation the best in our solar system and beyond; why can't we start taking care of our (Heavenly) Father's business?

We as supervisors/managers must always be mindful that it is our responsibility to help others who we supervise. This is not to say that we must treat all the same, but we must treat all of them and be just and fair (or right, since fair is ever-changing, depending on where you stand) in our dealing with them. Some come with more or different skills than others, and they, too, must understand that to whom much is given, much is required. They, too, must do their best to you as the leader and to the organization. If we can do this in our personal and spiritual lives, the world can only get better.

We as humans tend to think of power in terms of wealth, strength, violence, supremacy, and control over others who may be less fortunate. What if we were to look at this same strength of control in terms of faith? Faith in our Lord Jesus Christ, who looks and takes care of each one of us. The faith that what we have been blessed with, we must use for its intended purpose. As I have heard, to whom much is given, much is required. So, wealth and power are sure not to be confused with greed and seeking more power and more control through violence, but to share and give to those who are less fortunate.

Giving to those who are less fortunate and with goodwill toward all men is good during the holiday season and Christmas time, but this should be practiced each day, throughout the year, every year. Each day should be a time to give thanks to help others, for the bible says the poor will be with us always. So, with great power that has been bestowed on us by God himself should be used to further his kingdom and not our own sordid wants, needs and desires. Remember, this wealth does not have to be money, but it can be in time and service to further his kingdom. Let's start if we have not already and let us continue if we already have. Great powers and responsibilities start within each of us in terms of our personal responsibilities and end with our collective responsibility. Together they make up who we are and where we go in life. Look within yourselves for these great powers and you will see how it relates to our responsibilities to ourselves and each other.

You will be glad you did.

Personal Responsibility

The concept of responsibility encompasses not just our work life but also a variety of other areas of our lived experiences. Having personal integrity, acting in an ethical manner, and having a sense of moral duty to provide support and encouragement to individuals in our community are all components of this.

Personal Integrity: The concept of responsibility includes not just our work life but also a variety of other areas of our lived experiences. Having personal integrity, acting in an ethical manner, and having a sense of moral duty to provide support and encouragement to individuals in our community are all components of this.

Ethical Behavior: Ethical conduct, which includes making judgments and behaving in ways that are morally good and just, is still another component of responsibility that goes beyond personal integrity. The ability to comprehend the influence that one's activities have on other people and on society as a whole is essential for performing ethical conduct. Upholding ethical norms such as fairness, justice, and respect for the rights of others is a necessary component of this. Individuals contribute to a society that is fair and equitable on account of their ethical behavior.

Moral Duty to Support and Uplift Others: Also, we have a responsibility to help and encourage others around us if they are in need. Aspects of this include showing empathy and compassion, helping the downtrodden, and working to make our places of residence better. Essential to this idea is the realization of our interconnectedness and the participation in actions that improve the lives of others. One approach is to be there emotionally for those closest to you, whether that's via mentorship, volunteering, or charitable work.

Taking responsibility in a personal connection is owning up to your mistakes and the ways in which they affected other people. Being trustworthy and helpful is essential if you want to add to the stability and strength of these friendships.

A part of being responsible is being involved in the community and doing what you can to improve it. Some examples of what this may include are fighting for social justice and positive change and taking part in civic activities like voting and community service.

Collective Responsibility

In the context of a community or organization, the term "collective responsibility" refers to the shared accountability of all members for the activities and results accomplished by the group. This notion places an emphasis on the fact that the actions and choices of each member contribute to the establishment of the group's culture as well as its overall success.

Influence on Culture: Individuals have a tremendous impact on the culture of a community or organization by the behaviors that they take. Culture may be defined as the aggregate of values, beliefs, and behaviors that are held in common by a group of people. People contribute to the creation of a pleasant and welcoming atmosphere when they behave in a manner that demonstrates integrity, respect, and collaboration. On the other hand, unethical conduct such as dishonesty, disrespect, or selfishness may contribute to the development of a toxic environment. It is the dedication of each individual member to good acts that help to build and maintain a culture that is characterized by trust, cooperation, and mutual respect.

Enhancing Success: The success of the collective is directly proportional to the contributions made by each individual. When members of a team in an organization accept responsibility for their positions and carry out their responsibilities with diligence, it creates an environment that is conducive to overall productivity and effectiveness. An example of this would be individuals who go above and beyond their job requirements, assist their coworkers, and share their expertise in the workplace. These employees contribute to the development of an organization that is more dynamic and resilient. To a similar extent, persons who are actively involved in community activities and who provide support for community projects contribute to an improvement in the overall quality of life and well-being of the community.

Building Accountability: A further aspect of collective accountability is that members are responsible for holding each other accountable. Peer evaluations, feedback systems, and collaborative problem-solving are all examples of activities that may do this inside a company. When everyone in the group has the sense that they are accountable for the success of the group, they are more likely to take proactive measures to solve problems and assist one another in attaining objectives and standards. Because everyone is aware that their contributions are significant, this shared responsibility helps to cultivate a feeling of belonging and commitment among the members of the group.

Encouraging Ethical Behavior: Behavior that is ethical is encouraged when there is a feeling of group responsibility. In situations when people are aware that their activities have an effect on the whole group, they are more inclined to behave in a responsible and ethical manner. This shared philosophy contributes to the prevention of unethical behavior and fosters an environment that values honesty and equity. When workers in a company see their leaders and peers regularly following ethical norms, for instance, they are more inclined to follow suit, which results in the establishment of a solid basis for ethical policies and practices.

Strength and Ability to Adapt: The capacity of a community or organization to bounce back from adversity and adjust to new circumstances is enhanced by collective responsibility. When faced with tough circumstances; groups are able to come together, provide support for one another, and successfully traverse challenges when they have a strong sense of shared responsibility. This concerted effort has the potential to result in creative ideas as well as a group that is more powerful and unified.

Biloxi Management Pearl: "A wise man learns by the mistakes of others, a fool by his own." Latin Proverb

Scripture: "Cease, my son, to hear the instruction that causeth to err from the words of knowledge." (Proverbs 19:27)

Application of Biloxi Management Pearl to the Lesson:

Personal Observation:

"The art of being wise knows what to overlook." William James

This is a great quote, in my opinion, in that it gives credence to the old saying that I have heard said at least two ways: Rule number one is don't sweat the small stuff and rule number two is everything is small stuff. The other way I have heard it said is Rule number one is don't sweat the small stuff and rule number two is see rule number one.

In leadership roles, I have done this in trying to protect or create my craft. You must find your own style of leadership. How do you do this, simply by looking, learning, praying and observing? Pay close attention to those who supervised you and pay closer attention to your colleagues who are being supervised. Note what they are saying and why they are saying it. During conversations with your peers, ask why they feel that way about a decision that was made.

You will soon notice that you are learning from the mistakes of others. When the time comes for you to be in that leadership position, you will know first and secondhand what to do.

I have done this most of my career, you must remember that we all have a supervisor or someone above us. Even the president has Congress and the people, and believe it or not, even a dictator has someone he/she may not know who it is. Biblically speaking, God is always in control, no matter where we are on this earth.

I told you that the skillet was hot", I told you not to go down to that pond," I told you not to go there." I told you>>> We have heard that many times, and we have probably said it to our children, nephew, nieces, or just young people altogether. A hard head makes a soft behind", how can we forget that one and many more like it. Those and many more were things we heard as children, and we have told our children in hopes of them not making the same mistakes as we did. However, we didn't listen.

When we are young, we don't listen; it is not until we become older that we realize what our elders were saying and, in their own way, trying to help us back then. We were too busy thinking that they were trying to run our lives. I did not really understand that they were, but it was out of safety and concern. Remember when you said something to the effect, I will be glad when I grow up. I will stay up and out as long as I want when I want. What we come to realize is that staying up late, going out late and doing what we want, when we want is very overrated, at best. As children and some adults, we are fools. I remember telling my sons on several occasions, you do know that having bills in your name is a very overrated experience, and just wait, you will get it soon enough. This is especially so when they talked about wanting to have something that they weren't mature enough to handle or wanting to do this and/or that when I believed it was not in their best interest.

When we see others making a mistake, and we still try it, yes, we are fools, hard-headed, noncompliant and in some cases, just plain old stupid. In my younger days, I remember asking this young lady about a guy she was dating (Yes, I admit, because she did not want to date me, instead).We were friends, after all, so I asked her why she wanted to date a man who had never been married and had 4 children from their different mothers (I believe, or there about).Her reply was, because I thought those other women did not know what they were doing and that I could show them that I was the one and because I knew I was the one who could make him change. I started to find out that this was a common theme for some women back then and maybe now. So, why did I bring this up, and what does it have to do with management, etc.? Very good question, and the answer is we must look within ourselves. What makes us believe that by trying the same thing that the other supervisor/managers did and expecting it to work out for us, just because the other managers/supervisors did not know what they were doing? Thinking that I am the "perfect supervisor" and that is why they will do as I say.

There is a saying that it is a sign of insanity to do the same thing and expect a different result. So, when in doubt and you don't know who to listen to or when, remember (**Proverbs 3:5-6). Trust in the LORD with all thine heart; and lean not unto thine own understanding.** In all thy ways acknowledge him, and he shall direct thy paths.

So, even when you are tempted to go your own way or choose not to heed what others are saying, pray for guidance and then trust in Him (God). Our guardian angels come in many forms and fashions; God may be trying to tell you something just by learning from the mistakes of others.

It is never too late to learn, especially and more importantly, when it comes from the word of God.

Servant Leadership

Matthew 20:26-28: "But it shall not be so among you: but whosoever will be great among you, let him be your minister; And whosoever will be chief among you, let him be your servant: Even as the "Son of Man" came not to be ministered unto, but to minister, and to give his life a ransom for many."

According to **(Matthew 20:26-28)**, Jesus addresses His disciples in response to a discussion that they were having over which of them was the most outstanding. By showing that true leadership is defined by service to other people, Jesus challenges their old image of grandeur via the teachings that he imparted. As a mirror of His own life, which was marked by selflessness and sacrifice, Jesus emphasizes that in order to be really great, one must take on the role of a servant. This is a reflection of His own life.

Modern Leadership

What is Service Over Authority?

In order to emphasize that authentic leadership is defined by selflessness, Jesus reframes greatness as the act of putting the needs of others ahead of one's own. The contemporary leaders of today should not be concerned with their personal power but rather with the extent to which they can take their team. To create an environment in which every member has the opportunity to realize their full potential, it is necessary to place an emphasis on the growth and empowerment of team members. When leaders place a higher priority on the accomplishments of the community, empathy, and support than they do on individual ambition and control, they may be able to create a work atmosphere that is more enjoyable and productive. After adopting this servant leadership strategy, which is founded on the teachings of Jesus, leaders and their teams experience more success over the course of a longer period of time.

Comprehending the Real World

Empathetic Leadership: Leaders should actively listen to and understand their team members' needs, creating an environment of support and empathy. This involves not only hearing their concerns but also genuinely engaging with their perspectives and emotions. By doing so, leaders demonstrate that they value and respect their team members, fostering a sense of trust and loyalty. Providing timely feedback, recognizing achievements, and addressing issues compassionately are key aspects of this approach. When leaders prioritize empathy and support, they help build a positive workplace culture where employees feel appreciated and motivated, leading to increased satisfaction, productivity, and overall team cohesion.

Empowerment: Assisting team members in speaking out and taking the lead is essential for creating an inclusive and effective workplace. Providing resources, assistance, and opportunities for growth is one effective method to do this. Employees are empowered to increase their skills and confidence when they have access to training programs, mentoring, and professional growth initiatives. One way to help people feel like they belong is to make it easy for them to talk to one another and share their thoughts and opinions. Leaders may foster an inspiring, productive, and harmonious team by assisting members in their personal development and making sure their work is recognized and appreciated.

Sacrificial Leadership: Leaders, like Jesus, should be prepared to lay down their lives for their team, prioritizing the group's needs before their own. What this entails is putting the team's happiness and success ahead of your own. Being there for your team no matter what and making choices that are in the best interest of the group regardless of the personal cost are two ways leaders may show this. Inspiring their staff to likewise dedicate themselves to the organization's success and welfare, leaders create a culture of trust and loyalty by demonstrating this unselfish attitude.

How to Create a Service-Oriented Culture?

Leading by Example: Leaders may achieve greatness by serving others and building an encouraging, productive, and supportive work environment by modeling the servant leadership style shown by Jesus. In this method, leaders are urged to put their team's needs first, by creating a setting where workers are appreciated and given agency. Leaders may boost morale and foster strong, collaborative relationships by putting an emphasis on serving rather than dominating. A more united and inspired workforce, enhanced individual and team performance, and long-term, meaningful success for the company are all outcomes of this dedication to helping others.

Practical Steps: There are many ways in which leaders may put biblical foundations into practice to benefit their teams and communities. Leaders with more experience may help those with less experience improve professionally and personally by establishing mentoring programs. Promoting volunteerism has several benefits, including helping those in need, building stronger team relationships, and teaching empathy and purpose. Some real-world methods to help include volunteering, donating to good causes, and teaming up with neighborhood groups to complete service projects. Leaders may leave a lasting impression by helping their teams and communities, which is a hallmark of servant leadership.

The End

And he said unto me, My grace is sufficient for thee: for my strength is made perfect in weakness. Most gladly therefore will I rather glory in my infirmities, that the power of Christ may rest upon me.

(2 Corinthians 12:9 kjv)

1 Therefore being justified by faith, we have peace with God through our Lord Jesus Christ:

2 By whom also we have access by faith into this grace wherein we stand, and rejoice in hope of the glory of God.

3 And not only so, but we glory in tribulations also: knowing that tribulation worketh patience;

4 And patience, experience; and experience, hope:

(Romans 5:1-4 kjv)